First-time
VEGAN

First-time
VEGAN

Delicious dishes and simple switches
for a plant-based lifestyle

LEAH VANDERVELDT

RYLAND PETERS & SMALL

LONDON • NEW YORK

Designers Toni Kay, Paul Stradling
Commissioning Editor Alice Sambrook
Production Controller Mai-Ling Collyer
Editorial Director Julia Charles
Art Director Leslie Harrington
Publisher Cindy Richards

Food Stylist Emily Kydd
Prop Stylists Alexander Breeze,
Jennifer Kay

Indexer Vanessa Bird

Published in 2019 by
Ryland Peters & Small
20–21 Jockey's Fields
London WC1R 4BW
and
341 E 116th Street
New York, 10029

www.rylandpeters.com

10 9 8 7 6 5 4 3 2 1

Text copyright © Leah Vanderveldt 2019
The recipes in this book have been previously
published in *The New Nourishing* and *The
New Porridge*. Design and photographs
copyright © Ryland Peters & Small 2019.

ISBN: 978-1-78879-062-8

A CIP record for this book is available from
the British Library.
US Library of Congress CIP data has been
applied for.

Printed in China

NOTES

Both British (Metric) and American (Imperial plus US cups)
measurements are included in these recipes for convenience;
however it is important to work with one set of measurements
and not alternate between the two within a recipe.

All spoon measurements are level unless otherwise specified.

Ovens should be preheated to the specified temperatures. We
recommend using an oven thermometer. If using a fan-
assisted oven, adjust temperatures according to the
manufacturer's instructions.

When a recipe calls for the grated zest of citrus fruit, buy
unwaxed fruit and wash well before using. If you can only find
treated fruit, scrub well in warm soapy water before using.

Always use sterilized jars. For more information visit the Food
Standards Agency (FSA) website in the UK or the United
States Department of Agriculture (USDA) website in the US.

DISCLAIMER

The views expressed in this book are those of the author, but
they are general views only, and readers are urged to consult
a relevant and qualified specialist or physician for individual
advice before beginning any dietary regimen.

CONTENTS

HOW TO BEGIN

So you're interested in eating vegan — congratulations! Whether you've decided to go vegan for a specific cause or for your personal well-being, it's all good. Eating even just one vegan meal a day can help make positive changes to your health and to the health of the environment.

A WORD OF ADVICE

If you're thinking about going vegan for the first time, start gradually. Begin with one meal a day, then step it up to two (I love Mark Bittman's Vegan Before 6 idea – having a vegan breakfast and lunch, then a dinner that's more flexible). Once you get into this habit, you'll find that it's easy to go full days and weeks on the vegan track.

Just remember this doesn't have to be an all-or-nothing situation. Be kind to yourself and don't get discouraged if you can't always stick to your vegan goals. We're all human and we want to make changes to our lives from a place of love, not shame.

SO, WHAT DO I EAT?

While there's a lot of noise out there on what, when, and how to eat, I think the most agreed-upon premise for healthy eating is simply: eat more vegetables and plant-based foods. And that's what my approach to vegan cooking is all about – finding new and delicious ways of eating more vegetables, fruits, legumes, whole grains/pseudograins, nuts and seeds.

In this book you'll find great staples for vegan cooking – from basics sauces, plant-based proteins and simple vegetable prep, to sweet and savoury breakfasts, substantial meals and delicious desserts.

Eating vegan doesn't have to be difficult or time-consuming, but it is a bit of a mindset shift. Instead of basing your meals around an animal protein like eggs or chicken, you're going to start basing your meals around plants. I like to approach it from a place of adding more vegetables and plant-based proteins IN, rather than focusing on what I'm leaving out.

Shifting the way you think of meals is the key to not getting stuck in the 'what do I eat?' dilemma. I love starting with favourite takeout staples as a springboard for meal ideas. Is chicken tikka masala your go-to take out? Swap the chicken for chickpeas (see page 113). Love a burger? Give the Black Bean and Beet Burgers a go (see page 118). Craving nachos? Definitely try the vegetable-loaded version (see page 67).

People sometimes refer to the high cost of eating organic and vegan as a reason not to, which to me is silly. Meat and fish cost much more per weight than fresh vegetables, and waaay more than chickpeas, lentils or tofu (even organic varieties). It does, however, take some planning to make sure you eat all of the fresh produce you're buying. But when you pair seasonal vegetables and fruit with pantry staples, you'll find it's easy to both plan meals and cook on the fly.

MEAL PLANNING AND PREP

With just a little awareness and forethought, effective meal planning and prep will make your vegan diet so much easier to maintain. Following these steps should help get you started.

Step 1: Take stock. Start your planning by looking at what you have leftover that still needs using up and comparing it with your schedule for the week to determine how many meals you'll need to make or prep for.

Step 2: Decide on recipes. I like to pick 1–2 easy recipes for complete meals such as a one-pot soup, stew or curry that will make great leftovers for another lunch or dinner.

Step 3: Pick extra meal building blocks. Refer back to what you have in the pantry for grains and plant-based protein inspiration. Then pick 1 grain, 1 legume, 1 sauce and 2 vegetables to roast or prep (see The Basics, pages 10–35 for some inspiration). These will be the foundations for other, more throw-together style meals.

Step 4: Figure out what extras you need and shop. I love going to my local farmer's market for produce if I can make it there. If you're lacking the time or motivation to hit the market or grocery store, but grocery delivery is available to you, give that a try. Don't let your dislike of a crowded grocery store hold you back from cooking.

Step 5: Cook. Do this when you have a spare hour or two, or do it in 30 minute instalments in the earlier half of the week. Turn on music, a podcast or a TV show to make it more fun.

VEGAN SUBSTITUTES

While I'm a big fan of focusing on fresh produce and creating flavours with herbs, spices and cooking methods, sometimes you need a straight up vegan substitute. Here are some essentials to keep in mind:

Nutritional yeast If you're looking for a cheesy Parmesan-like savoury flavour, this is it. Nutritional yeast doesn't sound all that exciting but it brings both B vitamins and umami flavour to sauces, pastas and any meals that need a little extra something. I use it in the Walnut 'Breadcrumbs' (see page 33) for a flavour-packed topping.

Cheese Aside from handy nutritional yeast, there are some great nut-based cheeses available to buy now. In particular, I've found a delicious ricotta and a cream cheese made from almonds and cashews. Just keep an eye out for weird preservatives or flavourings – this stuff doesn't taste good and isn't worth it.

Protein Tofu (made from soybeans), tempeh (made from fermented soybeans) and legumes (like lentils, peas, black beans, chickpeas, etc.) are some of the best and easiest forms of vegan protein. Protein also comes from grains and pseudograins (like quinoa, millet and brown rice) and all nuts and seeds.

Aquafaba Aquafaba is the name for the water leftover from cooking chickpeas (you can use the stuff right from the can). It's a great egg white substitute and can be used in desserts like pavlova (see page 141), cakes, cocktails and to make vegan mayonnaise.

Mayonnaise You can DIY with aquafaba as mentioned above, or you can buy it ready-made. There are lots of good-quality vegan options out there now. As with anything pre-packaged, just check the labels for ingredients so you know exactly what you're getting.

Milk There are plenty of dairy alternatives available in supermarkets now, but you can also make your own if you have a decent blender (see pages 12–13). Almond and cashew milks are great neutral-flavoured milks for everyday, and coconut milk and cream are great for desserts.

Yogurt Like milk, there are now many good quality plant-based yogurts available to buy, made from soy milk, coconut, almonds and other nuts, with minimal additives. Test out a few different types to find your favourites.

A NOTE ON GETTING ENOUGH PROTEIN

One of the main concerns people have when thinking about adopting a vegan diet is whether it can provide enough protein. Our bodies use protein to repair cells and make new ones, hence we need to consume enough of it to stay generally healthy and feel energized throughout the day. And for many people, animal products such as chicken and eggs are the most obvious and easy neatly packaged protein sources.

The good news is, it's actually also very easy to get enough protein from sources other than animal products. It should be noted that each of us as individuals require differing ratios of nutrients depending on our body types and activity level. These things can fluctuate week by week, so pay attention to your hunger and energy levels and adjust as you go.

Creating well-balanced plant-based meals with plenty of variety is the real key to consuming enough protein as a vegan. Because many whole plant foods contain protein, a combination of them together can give you all the protein you require. Choose 2 or 3 of the following protein-rich ingredients to include in a meal:

Legumes Chickpeas, lentils, black beans, white beans, green peas, peanuts etc.
Soy Edamame beans, tofu and tempeh.
Grains & pseudograins Brown or black rice, farro, oats, quinoa, millet and amaranth.
Nuts Almonds, cashews, pecans, pistachios and walnuts.

Seeds Pumpkin seeds/pepitas, flax seeds/linseeds, hemp seeds, sunflower seeds, chia seeds and sesame seeds.
Dark leafy greens Swiss chard, kale, spinach, rocket/arugula and collard greens.

SOME USEFUL KITCHEN TOOLS

If you're just starting out on your vegan journey, you'll probably be spending more time on prepping vegetables than ever before. In addition to a sharp knife and vegetable peeler, here are some tools I've found useful:

Microplane grater Wonderful for mincing garlic and ginger very finely.
Spiralizer or julienne peeler Useful for making noodle-like strips of courgette/zucchini, butternut squash, beetroot/beet, carrot and sweet potato.
Mandoline This tool can really up your salad game by halving the cutting time and producing thin, uniform slices. Just watch your fingers!
Immersion blender So good for puréeing hot soups directly in the pan and for salad dressings and dips that just need a quick blitz.
High speed blender This has been a game changer for me; I never used to think the higher-end blenders were worth the price tag until I got one. I use mine for everything from nut milks (see page 13), to nut butters (see page 18), smoothies and sauces – it's pretty much replaced my food processor.

TRAVELLING WHILE VEGAN

The good news is, like food shopping, travelling as a vegan has become much easier in the past few years. Before heading to a new city, I enjoy researching spots that specialize in vegetable-forward food, there are so many truly incredible places out there. Don't limit yourself to strictly vegan places, instead seek out places that have vegan options available and are flexible to specific diets, so you get to try a wider array of new and delicious things.

All of that being said, airports still have a long way to go in terms of providing options, so I recommend bringing provisions. I tend to pack at least one thing from the following list in my carry-on bag:

Nut butters, nuts and seeds Individual packs of nut butter are great when hunger hits, as are lightly roasted nuts and seeds.

Fresh and dried fruit Great to mix with nut butters.

A whole avocado Grab a plastic spoon, a knife and a little packet of salt in the terminal, then cut your avo open and enjoy.

A prepared meal in a lunchbox with roasted vegetables, hearty greens and extra plant-protein such as Barbecue Black beans (see page 22) or Spicy Tofu (see page 21).

GET GOING!

My hope for this book is that it inspires you to eat more plants in new ways that get you excited. My favourite part of vegan cooking is the diversity of foods I start to get creative with and the flavours that I discover. Know that you can stick to your new vegan habit if you find things that you love to eat that happen to be vegan and make them regularly. I hope this book can help you with that.

Happy cooking!

THE BASICS

Your starter pack of vegan essentials – for mixing, matching and maximizing flavour and texture variation. These add-ons can take a vegan meal from just okay to crazy-good and make it easy to top up on that all-important protein.

NUT MILKS

Making your own nut milk sounds hard, but here are three recipes that ignore the rules about straining and excessive soaking in favour of simplicity.

LAZY ALMOND MILK

3 tablespoons almond butter

500 ml/2 cups water

pinch of sea salt

HEMP MILK

55 g/1/2 cup hemp seeds

500 ml/2 cups filtered water

pinch of sea salt

CASHEW MILK

120 g/1 cup raw cashews, soaked in 500 ml/2 cups water for at least 2 hours or overnight, then drained

3 dates, stoned/pitted and soaked

pinch of sea salt

500–750 ml/2–3 cups water (separate from the soaking water)

MAKES ABOUT 500 ML/ 2 CUPS

LAZY ALMOND MILK

In a blender, process all the ingredients on high for 1–3 minutes until the almond butter is well combined with the water. Store in the refrigerator in an airtight jar for up to 4–5 days and shake before using.

HEMP MILK

Put everything in a blender and purée until smooth. This can take a couple of minutes, depending on your blender. Store in an airtight jar in the refrigerator for up to 7 days and shake before using.

CASHEW MILK

Start by blending the soaked and drained cashews with the dates and salt into a fine paste, then gradually add 500 ml/2 cups water and blend until smooth. You can add more water for a thinner consistency. Store in the refrigerator in an airtight jar for up to 5 days and shake before using.

COCONUT WHIPPED CREAM

The dairy-free answer to whipped cream, a spoonful of this will make any dessert feel extra special.

400-g/14-oz. can full-fat coconut milk,
    cooled in the refrigerator overnight

1 teaspoon pure maple syrup

1/4 teaspoon pure vanilla extract
    or paste

MAKES ABOUT 125 ML/½ CUP

Put a mixing bowl in the freezer about 5 minutes before you start.

Scoop out the hardened coconut cream from the top of the can, reserving the coconut water for something else (like a smoothie), and place the cream in the chilled mixing bowl.

Whip, using an electric whisk or beaters, until light and airy with little to no clumps, about 1–2 minutes. Add the maple syrup and vanilla, and whisk again for about 1 minute more to distribute evenly. Use immediately or store in an airtight jar in the refrigerator for up to 3 days.

TOASTED COCONUT

With a satisfying crunch and deep coconut flavour, taking a little extra time to toast your coconut flakes is totally worth it. Use these to add texture and bite to breakfasts like porridge and granola.

45 g/1 cup large unsweetened dried coconut flakes

baking sheet lined with baking parchment

MAKES 45 G/1 CUP

Preheat the oven to 180°C (350°F) Gas 4.

Spread the coconut flakes out on the lined baking sheet. Bake for 3–5 minutes until golden. Watch the flakes closely, as they can burn very quickly.

Leave to cool. Store in an airtight jar or container at room temperature for up to 2 weeks.

SUNFLOWER SEED BUTTER

If you have a nut allergy or just want to mix things up with some seeds, give this sunflower seed butter a try. I add ground cinnamon and vanilla extract here to give it a rich and naturally sweet flavour.

280 g/2 cups raw shelled sunflower seeds

½ teaspoon pure vanilla extract

½ teaspoon ground cinnamon (optional)

pinch of sea salt

1 tablespoon neutral-tasting oil, such as grape seed oil or sunflower/safflower oil

MAKES ABOUT 300 G/ 1¼ CUPS

Preheat the oven to 180°C (350°F) Gas 4.

Place the seeds on a baking sheet in a single layer and bake in the preheated oven for 5–8 minutes until lightly toasted. Watch them closely as these can burn easily, especially if you have a hot oven.

Allow the seeds to cool completely before transferring to a food processor or high-speed blender. Add the vanilla, cinnamon and salt and blend. Once you have a rough paste (after 6–7 minutes of blending), slowly add the neutral oil while the blades are going.

Blend for 8–12 minutes in total, possibly more, depending on your machine. Have patience, you will get a seed butter eventually. You'll have to scrape down the sides a few times, to make sure everything is getting incorporated.

Store in the refrigerator in an airtight jar for up to a month.

NUT BUTTERS

Fancy nut butters can get expensive. With a blender or food processor and some patience, you can make your own.

HAZELNUT BUTTER

130 g/1 cup hazelnuts, skins removed

1 tablespoon neutral-tasting oil, such as grape seed oil or sunflower/safflower oil

1 teaspoon pure vanilla extract

pinch of sea salt

2 tablespoons unsweetened cocoa or cacao powder (optional)

MAKES ABOUT 150 G/ ¾ CUP

CASHEW BUTTER

240 g/2 cups raw cashews

pinch of sea salt

1 tablespoon neutral-tasting oil, such as grape seed oil or sunflower/safflower oil

MAKES ABOUT 250 G/ 1¼ CUPS

HAZELNUT BUTTER

Process the hazelnuts in a food processor or high-speed blender for 8–12 minutes, depending on your machine. First you'll get a fine powder, but continue blending until you get a denser, softened nut butter.

Add the oil, vanilla, salt and cocoa or cacao powder (if using) and process to combine for 2–4 minutes until smooth. Depending on your food processor or blender, the consistency may vary. Store in the refrigerator in an airtight jar for up to a month.

CASHEW BUTTER

Preheat the oven to 180°C (350°F) Gas 4.

Place the cashews on a baking sheet in a single layer and bake in the preheated oven for 6–9 minutes until lightly toasted. Keep an eye on them to make sure they don't burn.

Allow the cashews to cool completely before transferring to a food processor or high-speed blender. Add the salt and blend. Once you have a rough paste (after 6–7 minutes of blending), slowly add the neutral oil while the blades are going. Blend for 8–12 minutes in total, possibly more, depending on your machine. Have patience, you will get a nut butter eventually. You'll have to scrape down the sides a few times, to make sure everything is getting incorporated. Store in the refrigerator in an airtight jar for up to a month.

SPICY TOFU

This tofu is great to keep in the fridge to give a protein boost to salads, grain bowls and stir-fries throughout the week. Sriracha is pretty spicy, but mellows when it's in the oven.

400-g/14-oz. block of extra firm tofu

3 tablespoons tamari

1 tablespoon sriracha

1 tablespoon sesame oil

baking sheet, lined with baking parchment

SERVES 4-5

Remove the tofu from its packaging and drain. Wrap in paper towels and press with a weight, such as a heavy cookbook or baking sheet, for 5–10 minutes to remove excess moisture. The drier you get the tofu, the crispier it will become.

Preheat the oven to 200°C (400°F) Gas 6.

Meanwhile, put the tamari, sriracha and sesame oil in a medium-sized bowl. Mix together with a fork or whisk until well combined.

Cut the block of tofu into 2.5-cm/1-inch cubes and toss in the marinade. Let sit for about 15 minutes.

Scatter the tofu cubes onto the lined baking sheet and bake in the preheated oven for 15 minutes. Flip the tofu cubes with a spatula and return to the oven for another 10–15 minutes until crisp and browned in places. Remove from the oven and leave to cool before serving.

CRISPY CHICKPEAS

The key to extra crispy chickpeas is making sure they are as dry as you can get them before you combine them with olive oil and spices. These are great as a snack on their own or as a protein-packed topper for salads and bowls. You can mix up the flavour coating with different herb and spice combinations.

210 g/1½ cups cooked chickpeas, drained well

1 tablespoon olive oil

1 teaspoon smoked paprika

¼ teaspoon cayenne pepper (optional)

salt, to taste

SERVES 4

Preheat the oven to 200°C (400°F) Gas 6.

Dry the chickpeas on a clean kitchen cloth or paper towels to remove any excess moisture.

In a medium bowl, toss the dry chickpeas with the olive oil, spices and salt to taste. Spread out on a baking sheet and bake in the preheated oven for about 25–30 minutes, shaking the tray halfway through, until beginning to brown.

Remove from the oven and allow the chickpeas to cool on the baking sheet (they will continue to crisp up more during this time), before serving. Once fully cooled, the chickpeas will keep for 3–4 days in a sealed container in the fridge.

BARBECUE BLACK BEANS

I'm a sucker for a good barbecue sauce. This recipe captures the classic smokey-sweet taste with the help of smoked paprika, tomato purée/paste and maple syrup. It mixes with protein-filled black beans for a great addition to Mexican-style dishes.

avocado or olive oil, for frying
1 garlic clove, chopped
1 teaspoon smoked paprika
1/2 teaspoon ground cumin
1 x 400-g/14-oz. can black beans in their liquid
2 tablespoons tomato purée/paste
1 tablespoon pure maple syrup
60–120 ml/1/4–1/2 cup water or vegetable stock/broth
salt, to taste

SERVES 4

Heat a thin layer of oil in a large pan with high sides over a medium-high heat. Add the garlic and spices and cook, stirring, for 1 minute.

Add the black beans with their liquid and stir to coat in the spices. Add the tomato purée/paste, maple syrup, season with salt and stir. Turn the heat to medium-low, cover and simmer for 10 minutes. Add some water or vegetable stock/broth if the mixture looks dry. Remove from heat and stand, covered, for 10 minutes before serving.

pictured: page 20

HERB DRESSING

This dressing is great if you have a bunch of leftover herbs you're looking to use up. It's adaptable to what you have and it gives a bright freshness to everything you eat it with. If you want a creamier version, blend with 75 ml/1/3 cup soaked cashews.

20 g/1/2 packed cup fresh parsley
20 g/1/2 packed cup fresh coriander/cilantro leaves and stems
10 basil leaves
1 garlic clove, peeled
1 tablespoon hemp seeds
1 tablespoon fresh lemon juice
60 ml/1/4 cup olive oil

MAKES ABOUT 120 ML/1/2 CUP

Place all the ingredients along with 2 tablespoons of water in the bowl of a small food processor. Blend, scraping down the sides once or twice, for about 1–2 minutes, until smooth and very green.

MAPLE MUSTARD

Sweet, punchy and a little sharp. I love using a combination of smooth and wholegrain Dijon mustards to give this delicious dressing a little extra colour and texture.

4 tablespoons Dijon mustard
    (I used half smooth, half wholegrain)
2 tablespoons pure maple syrup
2 tablespoons olive oil
1 teaspoon salt

sterilized jar with a lid (optional)

MAKES ABOUT 120 ML/½ CUP

Whisk all the ingredients together with 2 tablespoons of water in a small bowl, or place all of the ingredients in the jar with a lid and shake vigorously to combine. Add more water to thin out, if desired.

BASIC VINAIGRETTE

Simple, easy and necessary. I use this one at least three times a week.

2 tablespoons apple cider vinegar
60 ml/¼ cup extra virgin olive oil
2 teaspoons Dijon mustard
¼ teaspoon salt
2–3 grinds of black pepper

sterilized jar with a lid (optional)

MAKES ABOUT 75 ML/⅓ CUP

Put everything together in the jar with a lid. Add 1 tablespoon of water, pop the lid on, and shake vigorously. Or, whisk everything together in a small bowl. Add another tablespoon or so of water until you reach the desired consistency.

PEANUT DRESSING

This sauce has a little kick and is great for dressing Asian-style dishes such as noodle bowls.

2 tablespoons tamari

2 tablespoons natural (no sugar added) smooth peanut butter

1 tablespoon fresh lime juice

2.5-cm/1-inch piece of fresh ginger, grated or finely chopped

1 garlic clove, finely chopped

1 teaspoon chilli/chili paste

MAKES ABOUT 120 ML/½ CUP

In a small bowl, whisk together all the ingredients with 2 tablespoons of water or more as needed. Or, purée with a stick blender or in a small food processor until smooth.

TAHINI-LEMON DRESSING

If you're new to tahini, give this dressing a try. It's great for when you're craving something creamy.

50 g/¼ cup tahini, mixed well

60 ml/¼ cup warm water

juice of half a lemon, plus extra to taste

1 small garlic clove, finely chopped or grated

salt and freshly ground black pepper

sterilized jar with a lid (optional)

MAKES ABOUT 120 ML/½ CUP

Combine all the ingredients (including a pinch of salt and pepper) in the jar with a lid and shake vigorously. Or, whisk everything together in a small bowl. Taste for seasoning and add more salt and/or lemon juice if necessary.

TAHINI-RANCH DRESSING

I used to love ranch dressing as a kid and wouldn't eat a salad that wasn't drowned in it. Today, I don't actually like the taste of most of the bottled varieties. This version has the requisite creaminess without the additives.

50 g/¹/₄ cup tahini, mixed well
60 ml/¹/₄ cup warm water
2 tablespoons finely chopped fresh chives
1 tablespoon finely chopped fresh parsley
1 teaspoon onion powder
1 teaspoon garlic powder
¹/₂ teaspoon dried dill
1 teaspoon pure maple syrup
freshly squeezed juice of half a lemon
¹/₂ teaspoon salt
few grinds of black pepper

MAKES ABOUT 175 ML/¾ CUP

In a small bowl, whisk together all the ingredients until well combined. Or, purée everything in a small food processor. Add a touch more water, if needed, to thin out to your desired consistency.

TAHINI-HARISSA DRESSING

Spicy, creamy and appropriate for dipping vegetables in, slathering on sandwiches or topping falafel with.

50 g/¹/₄ cup tahini, mixed well
1 small garlic clove, peeled
1 teaspoon harissa paste
¹/₂ teaspoon salt
1 tablespoon fresh lemon juice

sterilized jar with a lid (optional)

MAKES ABOUT 120 ML/¹/₂ CUP

Blend everything together with 60 ml/¹/₄ cup of water in a small food processor, or in the jar with a stick blender until smooth.

ROMESCO SAUCE

I love this sauce, made out of pantry staples, for its smoky richness.

60 g/½ cup cashews,
  soaked for at least
  an hour

200 g/1 cup roasted red
  peppers from a jar

1 garlic clove, peeled

2 tablespoons olive oil

1 tablespoon red wine
  vinegar

¼ teaspoon smoked
  Spanish paprika

¼ teaspoon cayenne
  pepper

½ teaspoon salt

*MAKES ABOUT
295 ML/1¼ CUPS*

Blend all the ingredients in a small food processor until smooth. Taste for seasoning; add more salt as needed.

BROCCOLI PESTO

Make this with that last crown of broccoli haunting your salad drawer.

1 small head of broccoli
  (including stems),
  chopped into
  small pieces

1 garlic clove, peeled

30 g/1 cup fresh basil,
  tightly packed

3–4 tablespoons olive oil

½ teaspoon nutritional
  yeast

¼ teaspoon salt, plus
  more to taste

*MAKES ABOUT
350 ML/1½ CUPS*

Steam or boil the broccoli in a little water for 3–5 minutes until tender. Drain and run under cold water. Combine the broccoli with the remaining ingredients in a small food processor and blend until smooth-ish. Adjust the seasoning to taste.

CHERMOULA

With salty olives and the brightness of lemon zest and juice, this sauce gives a little lift to grains or roasted veg.

120 ml/½ cup extra virgin olive oil

4 garlic cloves, roughly chopped

½ teaspoon ground coriander

½ teaspoon chilli flakes/hot red pepper flakes

¼ teaspoon ground cumin

¼ teaspoon paprika

15 g/½ cup fresh coriander/cilantro leaves and stems

15 g/⅓ cup fresh parsley leaves

½ teaspoon lemon zest

freshly squeezed juice of half a lemon

¼ teaspoon salt

35 g/⅓ cup whole pitted Kalamata olives,
  roughly chopped

MAKES ABOUT 235 ML/1 CUP

In a small saucepan, combine the oil and garlic over a medium-low heat. Cook for about 3–4 minutes until the garlic is sizzling, then let it sizzle for 1 minute.

Add the ground coriander, chilli flakes/hot red pepper flakes, cumin and paprika and stir. Turn off the heat and allow the mixture to cool in the pan.

Place the coriander/cilantro, parsley, lemon zest and juice, salt, olives and spiced garlic oil (along with the garlic) in a food processor (I use a mini one). Blend until everything is finely chopped and well combined.

Alternatively, finely chop all the ingredients and whisk together, adding the olive oil slowly.

CREAMY CHIPOTLE DIP

This sauce is becoming a fast favourite in our house. It's creamy, smoky and a little spicy. It's great on tacos and nachos.

75 g/⅓ cup tahini, mixed well

1 chipotle pepper in adobo sauce or ½ tablespoon chipotle paste

1 tablespoon adobo sauce from the pepper can (omit if using the paste)

1 tablespoon fresh lime juice

1 teaspoon pure maple syrup

½ teaspoon salt

1 garlic clove, peeled

MAKES ABOUT 235 ML/1 CUP

Place all the ingredients in a food processor and blend together with 75 ml/⅓ cup of water until smooth. Add more water, if needed, to reach the desired consistency.

GARLIC YOGURT DIP

A tastier alternative to sour cream.

215 g/1 cup plain unsweetened vegan yogurt

1 garlic clove, finely grated

¼ teaspoon salt

black pepper, to taste

1 tablespoon olive oil, plus more to serve

MAKES ABOUT 235 ML/1 CUP

In a small bowl, stir together the dip ingredients with a fork. Serve with additional olive oil and freshly ground black pepper, if desired.

BASIC AVOCADO DIP

This avocado dip is beyond simple to put together and adds a silky, vibrant green cloak to sautéed or roasted vegetables, grain bowls and greens, and it makes a wonderful dip for sweet potato fries.

1 avocado, peeled and pitted

juice of half a lemon or lime

small handful of fresh coriander/cilantro leaves

sea salt, to taste

MAKES ABOUT 175–235 ML/¾–1 CUP

Place the avocado, lemon or lime juice, coriander/cilantro leaves and a good pinch of sea salt in a food processor or blender. Blend to a smooth purée.

Add water a tablespoon at a time, blending again until you reach the desired consistency – I like mine thick enough for a dip but thin enough to drizzle. Taste and add extra sea salt, if desired.

CARAMELIZED ONIONS

Caramelized onions make everything better, in my opinion. If I've made something that's turned out a little meh, the best way I can think to spruce it up is with a little helping of caramelized onions. Best of all, they're so simple to make with just a few basic ingredients and some time.

2 tablespoons olive oil
2 large red onions, thinly sliced
1 tablespoon balsamic vinegar
salt, to taste

SPICY OPTION
1 teaspoon chilli flakes/hot red pepper flakes
1 teaspoon pure maple syrup

SERVES 4–6

Heat the olive oil in your largest frying pan/skillet or Dutch oven over a medium heat. Add the sliced onions, season with salt and stir to combine.

Cook, stirring occasionally, for 15–20 minutes, reducing the heat to medium-low if the onions are browning quickly. If the mixture gets dry, add a splash of water to keep things from sticking.

Stir in the balsamic vinegar and cook for another 10–15 minutes, until the onions are softened, sweet and a little sticky. If you are going for the spicy option, stir in the chilli flakes/hot red pepper flakes and maple syrup at the end of cooking.

COCONUT BACON BITS

I'm not going to pretend that coconut is a doppleganger for bacon, but it does make a convincing plant-based stunt double. It hits the right crunchy, smoky and salty notes that can make a salad pop.

1 tablespoon olive oil
1/2 teaspoon pure maple syrup
3/4 teaspoon smoked paprika
1 teaspoon salt
50 g/1 cup coconut flakes

baking sheet, lined with baking parchment

MAKES ABOUT 50 G/1 CUP

Preheat the oven to 180°C (350°F) Gas 4.

In a medium bowl, whisk together the olive oil, maple syrup, smoked paprika and salt.

Add the coconut flakes to the bowl and stir to coat in the mixture.

Spread out on the prepared baking sheet and bake in the preheated oven for 10 minutes. Allow to cool fully on the baking sheet before serving. Store in a sterilized glass jar in the fridge for up to a month.

DUKKAH

This spice and nut blend is a great way to add crunch and flavour to dishes. I love it combined with a few tablespoons of extra virgin olive oil as a dip for sourdough bread.

35 g/¹/₄ cup pistachios, roughly chopped
35 g/¹/₄ cup almonds, roughly chopped
1 tablespoon cumin seeds
1 tablespoon coriander seeds
1 tablespoon sesame seeds
1 teaspoon sea salt
1 teaspoon freshly ground black pepper
¹/₂ teaspoon chilli flakes/hot red pepper flakes

MAKES ABOUT 90 G/¾ CUP

Heat a large frying pan/skillet over a medium heat. Add the pistachios and almonds and dry toast them for about 5 minutes, tossing occasionally, until they're starting to turn golden and fragrant. Transfer to a plate.

In the same pan, toast the cumin seeds, coriander seeds and sesame seeds for about 2–4 minutes over a medium-low heat, until fragrant.

Combine the toasted nuts and seeds, salt, pepper and chilli flakes/hot red pepper flakes in the bowl of a small food processor and pulse carefully until just finely chopped – you don't want a fine powder, you're looking for pieces that lend a bit of crunch. Store in a sterilized glass jar in the fridge for up to a month.

pictured: page 31

SAVOURY-SWEET GRANOLA

I know granola on a green salad or as a savoury garnish sounds weird, but for me, it adds a good amount of crunch and flavour.

95 g/1 cup rolled oats
140 g/1 cup pumpkin seeds/pepitas
3 tablespoons flax seeds
1 tablespoon fresh thyme leaves
¹/₂ teaspoon salt
3 tablespoons olive oil
2 tablespoons pure maple syrup

baking sheet, lined with baking parchment

MAKES ABOUT 250 G/2 CUPS

Preheat the oven to 160°C (325°F) Gas 3.

Mix together the oats, pumpkin seeds/pepitas, flax seeds, thyme and salt in a medium bowl.

In another small bowl or pourable measuring cup, combine the olive oil and maple syrup and stir together. Pour the olive oil mixture onto the oat mixture and stir until everything is well coated.

Spread the oats out on the prepared baking sheet. Bake in the preheated oven for 35–40 minutes until golden. Rotate the baking sheet halfway through the cooking time. Let the granola cool completely on the baking sheet. Store in a sterilized glass jar in the fridge for up to a month.

pictured: page 31

WALNUT 'BREADCRUMBS'

This crunchy topping is reminiscent of Parmesan breadcrumbs. Use as a topping to add texture to pasta, salads, veggies or polenta.

2 tablespoons olive oil
1 garlic clove, finely chopped
1/2 teaspoon sea salt
140 g/1 cup walnut halves
   (or a combo of walnuts and cashews)
1 teaspoon nutritional yeast

baking sheet, lined with baking parchment

SERVES 4–6

Preheat the oven to 180°C (350°F) Gas 4.

Combine all the ingredients in a small food processor. Pulse a few times to combine and roughly chop the nuts, until you have a coarse breadcrumb-like texture. (You can do this with a knife, too, it will just take a little longer.)

Spread the mixture out on the prepared baking sheet. Bake in the preheated oven for 9–12 minutes until the walnuts are toasted.

Allow to cool fully before using. Store in a sterilized jar in the fridge for up to 2 weeks.

GARLIC GREENS

If you have a big bunch of greens languishing in the fridge drawer, give them a clean and turn them into garlicky goodness. I like making a big batch to toss into grain bowls, soups and stews for a boost in leafy nutrients.

olive oil, for frying
3 garlic cloves, finely chopped
2 bunches of hearty greens like kale or Swiss chard, cleaned, stems removed*, and thinly sliced into ribbons
1/4 teaspoon chilli flakes/hot red pepper flakes

SERVES 4

Heat a thin layer of olive oil in a large pan with high sides over a medium heat. Add the garlic and cook for 1 minute, stirring.

*If using Swiss chard, you can sauté the stems too. Finely chop the stems separately from the leaves. Add the stems to the hot pan first and cook for 2 minutes, stirring once or twice until softened. Add the leafy greens and cook for 2–3 minutes, stirring to distribute the heat, until wilted.

Remove from the heat and stir in the chilli flakes/hot red pepper flakes before serving.

pictured: page 34

5-SEED SLAW

This colourful slaw gets extra crunch and flavour from toasted seeds.

1 tablespoon sesame seeds

1 tablespoon pumpkin seeds/pepitas

1 tablespoon sunflower seeds

1 teaspoon cumin seeds

1 tablespoon poppy seeds

1 teaspoon Dijon mustard

juice of ½ lemon

2 tablespoons olive oil

¼ head of red cabbage, finely sliced using a mandoline or knife

60 g/1 cup kale, stems removed and shredded

1 large carrot, grated or peeled with a julienne peeler

small handful of fresh coriander/cilantro or parsley leaves, roughly chopped

salt, to taste

SERVES 4

Heat a medium frying pan/skillet over a medium heat. Add the sesame seeds, pumpkin seeds/pepitas, sunflower seeds, cumin seeds and poppy seeds. Dry toast for about 5–6 minutes, until fragrant and the sesame seeds are beginning to brown. Transfer the seeds to a plate and allow time to cool fully.

In a large bowl, combine the Dijon mustard, lemon juice and olive oil. Season with salt to taste and whisk quickly with a fork.

In the same bowl, add the cabbage, kale, carrot and fresh herbs and toss to evenly coat everything in the dressing. Add the toasted cooled seeds and toss again.

PAN-GRILLED BROCCOLI

I like to slice broccoli almost like broccoli 'steaks' for this, cutting them lengthwise. You want to partially caramelize the broccoli in the pan, so try not to toss or stir the pan in the first few minutes of cooking.

1–2 tablespoons olive oil

1 head of broccoli, with the tough bottom stem trimmed off and sliced into 1.5-cm/½-inch–2-cm/ ¾-inch thick pieces

2 garlic cloves, finely chopped or grated

salt, to taste

SERVES 4

Heat enough olive oil to cover the bottom of a large frying pan/skillet with a lid over a medium-high heat. Add the broccoli, distributing the pieces in an even layer. Season with salt.

Cover with a lid and cook for 4 minutes, without stirring, allowing the bottom to caramelize.

Add 120 ml/½ cup of water and the garlic and stir, flipping the broccoli slices as you do so. Cover again and cook for another 3 minutes until tender and caramelized on both sides.

BREAKFAST

Mornings are brighter, livelier and more fun with a good breakfast. Luckily, it is one of the more easily adaptable categories for vegans, with fresh fruit, oats and toast all lending themselves to natural and delicious plant-based options. I've also given you a couple of recipes for those mornings when you want something a bit different or more substantial.

CLASSIC BIRCHER MUESLI

Call it what you will — overnight oats, overnight porridge, etc. — I consider it bircher muesli when there's grated apple involved. This is porridge's summer outfit, to be enjoyed cold with fresh fruit and coconut yogurt.

95 g/1 cup rolled/old-fashioned oats

1 tablespoon flax seeds/linseeds

¼ teaspoon ground cinnamon

pinch of salt

1 firm eating apple (such as Granny Smith, Pink Lady, or Honeycrisp), cored and grated, along with any juices

250 ml/1 cup almond or coconut milk (or half water, half dairy-free milk of your choice)

1 teaspoon freshly squeezed lemon juice

1 teaspoon pure maple syrup

TOPPINGS
coconut yogurt

sliced fresh stone fruit – ideal when peaches, nectarines, apricots, and even cherries are in season

toasted flaked/sliced almonds

SERVES 2

Combine all the ingredients (except the toppings) together in a bowl and stir well to combine. Either cover the bowl or transfer to individual serving jars, and pop in the refrigerator overnight.

When you're ready to serve, top with 1 scoop of coconut yogurt per serving, fruit and toasted almonds, if you like.

CHOCOLATE AND COCONUT GRANOLA

If you love your breakfast on the sweet and crunchy side, making your own granola is one of the easiest and most satisfying things you should master. This version made with cacao tastes like grown-up Coco Pops.

190 g/2 cups rolled/old-fashioned oats

80 g/1 cup flaked/sliced almonds (substitute sunflower or pumpkin seeds for a nut-free version)

4 tablespoons cacao powder

2 tablespoons chia seeds

½ teaspoon sea salt

1 tablespoon maca powder (optional)

60 ml/¼ cup melted coconut oil

60 ml/¼ cup pure maple syrup

45 g/1 cup coconut flakes

baking sheet lined with baking parchment

MAKES ABOUT 500 G/ 3½ CUPS

Preheat the oven to 160°C (325°F) Gas 3.

In a large mixing bowl, combine the oats, almonds, cacao powder, chia seeds, salt and maca (if using). Mix together to distribute the cacao evenly.

In a pourable glass measuring jug/cup, combine the oil and maple syrup, and whisk together with a fork. Pour the wet ingredients into the dry and mix together until the oats are evenly coated.

Spread out in an even layer on the prepared baking sheet and bake in the preheated oven for 20 minutes. Take out the sheet, rotate it 180 degrees, sprinkle the coconut flakes on top and bake for another 15–20 minutes.

Note: If you smell burning at any point, take out the baking sheet to cool a little, stir the mixture and turn the oven down slightly. Return to the oven for the remainder of the cooking time or a little less.

Remove from the oven and leave to cool completely on the baking sheet – this is when it will really crisp up and get its crunch. Once cooled, break into pieces and store in an airtight jar at room temperature for up to 2 weeks, or in the refrigerator for up to 1 month.

CLASSIC MIXED OATMEAL PORRIDGE

This genius yet simple combination of coarse oatmeal/steel-cut oats and rolled/old-fashioned oats came to me by way of April Bloomfield in her book, 'A Girl and Her Pig'. It gives a creamy, yet textured consistency that is super satisfying.

70 g/½ cup coarse oatmeal/
steel-cut oats

50 g/½ cup rolled/old-fashioned
oats

2 teaspoons apple cider vinegar

500 ml/2 cups water, plus more
for soaking

250 ml/1 cup dairy-free milk of
your choice (store-bought or
see pages 12–13)

¾ teaspoon salt

OPTIONAL TOPPINGS
berry compote

Toasted Coconut (see page 14)

sliced fresh fruit (such as
banana, strawberries or kiwi)

chopped dried fruit (such as
cranberries, pineapple or
papaya)

add-ons for texture (such as
pistachios, chia seeds,
freeze-dried raspberries
or blueberry powder)

brown sugar or pure maple syrup

SERVES 2–3

The night before, combine both types of oatmeal/oats with enough water to cover them by about 5 cm/2 inches and the apple cider vinegar. Leave to sit at room temperature for at least 8 hours.

The next morning, drain the oats and rinse them. Transfer to a medium saucepan and add the water, milk and salt.

Bring to the boil, then reduce to a simmer. Cover with the lid slightly ajar and cook for 10–15 minutes, stirring occasionally. You want most of the liquid to be absorbed but the mixture should be loose and not gluey. If it's a little too thick for your liking, add more water and milk, and stir in, cooking for a couple of minutes more.

Serve with your desired toppings.

GREEN SMOOTHIE BOWL with peanut butter and banana

I know smoothies aren't the first thing that come to mind when you think of a satisfying meal, but hear me out on this one. The change of vessel to a bowl allows your smoothie to be enjoyed sitting at the table, spoon in hand, with copious amounts of toppings for added bite and flavour. For smoothie bowls, I look for a thicker texture, so blending can take longer than normal, but it's worth the wait. This one is refreshing, yet rich and creamy in a way that makes me crave it nearly every summer morning.

120 ml/½ cup almond milk

220 g/1½ cups frozen spinach (or 2 big handfuls of the fresh stuff)

1 frozen banana, broken into pieces

75 g/½ cup frozen mango chunks

1–2 tablespoons smooth peanut butter

OPTIONAL ADD-INS

1 teaspoon coconut oil

1 tablespoon flax seeds

1 tablespoon chia seeds

OPTIONAL TOPPINGS

granola

cacao nibs

coconut flakes

extra peanut butter

fresh fruit

SERVES 1

Pour the almond milk into the base of a blender. Add the spinach, banana and mango and start to blend at high speed. As the mixture is blending, pause once or twice to scrape down the sides with a rubber spatula to make sure that everything is well incorporated.

When the mixture is smooth, stop the blender, then add the peanut butter and any optional add-ins.

Blend again until everything is smooth and thick. Pour the smoothie into a bowl to serve and finish with your chosen toppings.

BLUEBERRY OVERNIGHT OAT SMOOTHIE

This is a smoothie-overnight oats hybrid, with the blended berries and coconut milk mixed with the oats to soak. Don't forget to add the maple syrup, to give it the right balance of sweet and tart.

190 g/1 cup frozen blueberries

250 ml/1 cup coconut milk

1 tablespoon pure maple syrup

pinch of salt

95 g/1 cup rolled/old-fashioned oats

1 tablespoon chia seeds

OPTIONAL TOPPINGS
toasted flaked/sliced almonds or almond butter

fresh fruit, such as cherries, blueberries or figs

sprinkling of dried blueberry powder

SERVES 1–2

Combine the frozen blueberries, coconut milk, maple syrup and salt in a blender and process until smooth. In a large jar or container with a lid, combine the oats and chia seeds. Pour the blueberry milk mixture over the oats and stir everything to combine. Pop the lid on and place in the refrigerator overnight.

The next day, portion the oat smoothie into bowls or jars, add the toppings and enjoy.

CHAI AND TURMERIC PORRIDGE

I'm always trying to sneak turmeric into as many dishes as I can. This root has some serious nutritional cred, with a slew of studies backing its anti-inflammatory properties. And with its vibrant yellow-gold hue, I can't help but be drawn to it. Using it alongside chai spices in my morning oats is an easy way to fit it into my day. This porridge is made with a combination of rolled/old-fashioned oats and buckwheat groats but if you can't find buckwheat, you can use all rolled oats instead.

45 g/½ cup rolled/old-fashioned oats

80 g/½ cup buckwheat groats (untoasted)

½ teaspoon ground cinnamon

½ teaspoon ground turmeric

½ teaspoon ground ginger

¼ teaspoon ground cardamom

¼ teaspoon ground nutmeg

⅛ teaspoon ground cloves

salt, to taste

475 ml/2 cups boiling water

235 ml/1 cup almond or coconut milk, plus extra to serve if needed

½ teaspoon vanilla extract

1 banana, sliced

TO SERVE
toasted flaked/slivered almonds

chopped figs, berries or extra banana

SERVES 2

Combine the oats and buckwheat in a medium saucepan with a lid. Add all the spices, season with salt to taste and stir until everything is well mixed together.

Pour in the boiling water, almond or coconut milk and vanilla, then bring to the boil.

Reduce to a simmer and cook with the lid on for about 10 minutes, stirring occasionally until the oats are soft and most of the liquid has been absorbed.*

Stir in the banana slices and cook for an additional 10 minutes, until they're softened and smell sweet. Serve with additional almond milk and a topping of toasted flaked/slivered almonds and fresh fruit.

*Alternatively, to save time in the morning you can prepare the oats the night before: simmer for 5 minutes, then remove from the heat and cover with a lid. Let the oats soak overnight at room temperature or in the fridge. In the morning, add a sliced banana to the oats. Bring back up to a bubble, adding a little more water or almond milk to loosen. Once heated through and creamy and the bananas are fragrant, you're ready to go.

EVERYTHING AVOCADO TOAST

Everything bagels are famous in New York – they're covered in a flavourful combination of seeds and alliums and in my opinion, they're the best type of bagel. When I lived in Sydney, it was pretty much impossible to find anything comparable to a New York bagel, so my Everything Bagel Spice Mix became an easy way to get a little taste of home. Combined with avocado and spring onions/scallions, this is pretty much all of my favourite breakfasts rolled into one.

2 large (or 4 small) slices of sourdough, whole-grain or sprouted grain bread

1 avocado, peeled, pitted and roughly chopped

1 spring onion/scallion, finely sliced

Everything Bagel Spice Mix (below)

SERVES 2

EVERYTHING BAGEL SPICE MIX

1 tablespoon sesame seeds

1 tablespoon poppy seeds

1 tablespoon dried garlic granules

1 tablespoon onion powder or dried onion

2 teaspoons sea salt

MAKES ABOUT 4 TABLESPOONS

Toast the bread to your liking, then top with the avocado, dividing it evenly between each slice. Use a fork to mash the avocado, pressing it into the toast. Sprinkle with the sliced spring onion/scallion and finally with some of the Everything Bagel Spice Mix.

For the Everything Bagel Spice Mix: toast the sesame seeds in a dry frying pan/skillet over a medium-low heat for about 5 minutes until turning golden. Watch them carefully, as they can burn easily. Remove from heat and allow to cool for about 5 minutes.

Put all the seeds and flavourings together in a small jar and shake to combine. The spice mix will keep for up to 6 months in the jar with a lid. It's also a great flavour and texture boost on salads, quinoa/grains, hummus and baked into savoury bread or muffins.

ULTIMATE BREAKFAST SANDWICH

I have a deep love for New York delis and the delicious breakfast sandwiches that are served in them. It's something that can't quite be replicated out of the Long Island/NYC/New Jersey area – like bagels and pizza by the slice. When I began thinking of a totally vegan version of a breakfast sandwich, I couldn't really wrap my head around it when I took away the egg and the cheese. But then I thought about the essence of a good breakfast sandwich, which is warming, rich and filling. This breakfast sandwich is all that. It's got creamy elements, as well as substantial carb-y ones, and has enough tang from harissa and barbecue sauce to keep it interesting.

1 butternut squash, peeled

1 avocado, peeled and pitted

1 tablespoon freshly chopped coriander/cilantro (optional)

4 English muffins (I love the Ezekiel sprouted ones)

salt, to taste

TO SERVE
Tahini-harissa Dressing (see page 25)

barbecue sauce

baking sheet, oiled

SERVES 4

Preheat the oven to 200°C (400°F) Gas 6.

Slice the neck or handle part of the butternut squash into 1.5-cm/½-inch thick rounds (save the hollowed-out base of the squash for another recipe). Spread the rounds out on the prepared baking sheet and season with salt to taste. Roast in the preheated oven for 30 minutes, flipping about halfway through, until golden and tender.

In a medium bowl, lightly mash the avocado with a pinch of salt and the chopped coriander/cilantro (if using).

When you're ready to serve, split and toast the English muffins. Spread the Tahini-Harissa Dressing on one half of each, top that with a butternut round or two and drizzle with barbecue sauce.

Spread the mashed avocado on the other half of each English muffin and sandwich everything together.

SWEET OR SAVOURY BREKKIE SWEET POTATOES

Here are two recipes to help you break out of a plant-based breakfast rut. I'd suggest baking a batch of a few sweet potatoes at the same time so you have them ready to go for the week. Mix it up with these sweet and savoury fillings.

1 small sweet potato, scrubbed clean and poked with a fork a couple of times

SWEET BREKKIE SWEET POTATO

1–2 teaspoons pure maple syrup

1 tablespoon almond butter

pinch of ground cinnamon

2 big spoonfuls of coconut yogurt

handful of fresh berries

handful of granola

SAVOURY BREKKIE SWEET POTATO

½ avocado, peeled and pitted

1 tablespoon freshly chopped coriander/cilantro

salt, to taste

pinch of chilli flakes/hot red pepper flakes or dash of hot sauce, plus extra to serve

olive oil

40 g/¼ cup canned black beans, drained and rinsed

SERVES 1

Preheat the oven to 200°C (400°F) Gas 6.

Put the sweet potato on the oven rack and bake in the preheated oven for about 45–60 minutes, until soft to the touch. Allow to cool a little. Note: You can do this step ahead of time and make a whole batch for the week, then reheat them in the microwave or in the oven right before serving.

Slice the warm potato open lengthwise and lightly mash the flesh with a fork.

SWEET BREKKIE SWEET POTATO

Drizzle the open warm potato with maple syrup and almond butter, then sprinkle with cinnamon. Top with coconut yogurt, berries and granola to finish.

SAVOURY BREKKIE SWEET POTATO

In a bowl, roughly mash the avocado flesh with the coriander/cilantro, a little salt and chilli flakes/hot red pepper flakes or hot sauce.

Top the open warm potato with a drizzle of olive oil, the mashed avocado and black beans. Serve with extra hot sauce, if desired.

SNACKS & LIGHT MEALS

Dishes that involve dipping, crunching and extra toppings make the best kind of snacks. Just because you have chosen to eat a plant-based diet doesn't mean you should have to miss out on grazing when you are a little hungry or building yourself an amazing sandwich.

SWEET TOASTS

I love the creativity that comes from combining a few things on a piece of toast. The following are intended more as inspiration than recipes.

HAZELNUT CHOC SPREAD

130 g/1 cup hazelnuts

2 tablespoons melted coconut oil

2 tablespoons pure maple syrup

2 tablespoons cocoa powder

1 teaspoon vanilla extract

pinch of sea salt

2 slices of bread

sliced strawberries, to serve

toasted hazelnuts, roughly chopped, to serve (optional)

SERVES 1 (WITH LEFTOVER CHOC SPREAD)

PEANUT BUTTER AND BERRY

2 slices of bread

2 tablespoons peanut butter

50–60 g/⅓–½ cup fresh berries or thawed frozen berries

pure maple syrup, to serve

hemp seeds, to serve

SERVES 1

BANANA AND SEED

2 slices of bread

2 tablespoons almond butter

1 banana, sliced into rounds

½ teaspoon hemp seeds

½ teaspoon chia seeds

1 teaspoon pumpkin seeds/ pepitas

SERVES 1

HAZELNUT CHOC SPREAD

Preheat the oven to 180°C (350°F) Gas 4.

Spread the nuts out on a dry baking sheet. Pop in the preheated oven for 5 minutes, shake the tray and roast for another 5 minutes until lightly toasted. If the skins are on the hazelnuts, cover the baking sheet with a kitchen towel and let cool for about 5–10 minutes before rubbing as many skins off as possible – getting about three quarters off is a win here, some are very stubborn. Process in a high speed blender for about 5–8 minutes until you get a dense, softened nut butter.

Add the melted coconut oil, syrup, cocoa powder, vanilla and sea salt and blend for 1–2 minutes until fairly smooth.

Toast the bread, then spread with the chocolate spread and top with strawberries and toasted hazelnuts, if desired. Leftover choc spread will keep well in the fridge for 2 weeks.

PEANUT BUTTER AND BERRY

Like PB&J but way better. Toast the bread to your desired toastiness. Slather on peanut butter. Top with berries, a drizzle of maple syrup and a sprinkle of hemp seeds.

BANANA AND SEED

Toast the bread to your desired toastiness. Spread generously with almond butter. Top with banana slices and sprinkle on the seeds.

SAVOURY TOASTS

These toasts make properly satisfying, substantial snacks at any time of day. A fresh sturdy bread with a good crust is best.

ROASTED CARROT AND HUMMUS

4 carrots

olive oil for roasting, plus extra for serving

2 slices of bread

1 garlic clove, cut in half

60 g/¼ cup Hummus (see page 64)

3 teaspoons Dukkah (see page 32)

2 teaspoons freshly chopped parsley

salt and freshly ground black pepper, to taste

SERVES 2

PEAS AND SPINACH

olive oil for frying, plus extra for serving

1 garlic clove, finely chopped

125 g/1 cup frozen peas, thawed

large handful of baby spinach

1 teaspoon lemon juice, plus extra to taste

2 large slices (or 4 small) of sourdough

1 garlic clove, cut in half

salt and freshly ground black pepper, to taste

vegan soft cheese or capers (optional), to serve

SERVES 2

ROASTED CARROT AND HUMMUS

Preheat the oven to 220°C (425°F) Gas 7.

Peel and roughly chop the carrots and toss with a splash of olive oil and a big pinch of salt. Place on a baking sheet and roast in the preheated oven for 25–30 minutes until golden and brown at the edges.

Toast the bread to your liking. Rub the warm bread with the half garlic clove.

Spread the bread with hummus and top with roasted carrots, dukkah and parsley. Drizzle with olive oil and season with salt and pepper.

PEAS AND SPINACH

In a medium frying pan/skillet, heat a thin layer of oil over a medium heat. Add the garlic and stir-fry for 20–30 seconds before adding the peas and spinach. Cook, stirring regularly, until everything is warmed through and the spinach has wilted, about 3 minutes. Season with salt and lemon juice and remove from the heat.

Mash the pan contents lightly with a fork or potato masher, or pulse everything in a food processor or blender. You're looking for a texture that is somewhere between a smooth purée and completely whole, so that the peas can stay atop the toast without rolling off.

Meanwhile, toast the bread to your desired shade of toastiness. Rub the warm bread with the cut sides of the garlic clove.

Spread the pea mixture on the toast. Top with vegan soft cheese and/or capers and black pepper.

TOMATO AND WHITE BEANS

2 tablespoons olive oil

3 large garlic cloves (or 5 small), finely chopped

1 tablespoon finely chopped fresh sage

1 x 400-g/14-oz. can chopped tomatoes

1 x 400-g/14-oz. can white beans, drained and rinsed

chilli flakes/hot red pepper flakes (optional)

salt, to taste

2–3 slices of toasted bread, flatbread or pita, to serve

SERVES 2–3

TOMATO AND WHITE BEANS

Heat the olive oil in a medium frying pan/skillet over a medium heat. Add the garlic and sage and sauté for 30 seconds until fragrant.

Stir in the tomatoes and white beans, then season with salt. Reduce the heat to low and cook, covered, for 10–15 minutes, stirring once or twice. Add a small splash of water if the pan dries out at any point.

Stir in chilli flakes/hot red pepper flakes (if using) and remove from the heat. Serve warm with toasted bread of your choice.

OVEN-BAKED ROSEMARY CRISPS/CHIPS

DIY oven crisps/chips are way prettier than the ones that come in a package. I highly recommend using a mandoline for slicing your beetroots/beets and potatoes because if they're not thin enough, they won't crisp up. I mention salt to taste (instead of an exact amount) because I find it easier to use a salt shaker here to distribute the salt in smaller quantities. Try serving these tasty crisps/chips with any of the Hummus recipes on pages 64–65 for dipping.

2 small-medium beetroot/beets

1 sweet potato, white potato or purple potato

olive oil, for brushing

1 tablespoon fresh rosemary leaves, finely chopped

salt, to taste

any of the Hummus recipes (see pages 64–65), to serve

2 baking sheets, brushed with oil

SERVES 3–4

Preheat the oven to 190°C (375°F) Gas 5.

Slice the beetroot/beets and potato very thinly (preferably with a mandoline).

Arrange the individual beetroot/beet and potato slices on the prepared baking sheets, giving each slice plenty of space.

Lightly brush the vegetables with a little olive oil. Sprinkle with the rosemary and season with salt to taste.

Bake in the preheated oven for 10–13 minutes, watching them carefully to make sure they don't burn. Remove from the oven and let the crisps/chips cool on the sheets before transferring to a serving plate or bowl. Repeat with any remaining vegetables as necessary. Serve with a big bowl of hummus for dipping, if you like.

BASIC HUMMUS

Start with this base, then add other ingredients to make your own signature flavour combinations.

210 g/1½ cups cooked chickpeas or 1 x 400-g/14-oz. can chickpeas, drained and rinsed

2 heaped tablespoons tahini

juice of half a small lemon

1 small garlic clove, peeled

3–4 tablespoons ice-cold water

salt, to taste

SERVES 4–6

Put the chickpeas, tahini, lemon juice and garlic in a food processor. Add salt to taste. Purée for 1–3 minutes, scraping down the sides once or twice with a rubber spatula as you go.

Add 2–3 tablespoons of ice cold water to the mixture to help give it a smooth but fluffy texture. Add more ice cold water as needed until you reach the desired consistency.

SPICY GREEN HUMMUS

olive oil for frying, plus extra to serve

1 small garlic clove, chopped

1 jalapeño, seeds and inner ribs discarded, chopped

70 g/½ cup canned chickpeas, drained and rinsed

60 g/½ cup shelled edamame beans

2 heaped tablespoons tahini

juice of half a lime

15 g/½ packed cup coriander/cilantro, plus extra to serve

3–4 tablespoons ice cold water

salt, to taste

SERVES 4–6

In a frying pan/skillet, heat 1 tablespoon olive oil over a medium heat. Add the garlic and jalapeño and cook for about 5 minutes until softened. Remove from the heat and stand for 5 minutes.

Place everything except the cold water (including the jalapeño, garlic and cooking oil) in a food processor and blend, scraping down the sides once or twice. Add the ice-cold water slowly until the texture is smooth and fluffy. Serve topped with olive oil and coriander/cilantro, if desired.

BUTTERNUT AND HARISSA HUMMUS

1 tablespoon olive oil

2 garlic cloves, finely chopped

½ teaspoon ground cumin

140 g/½ cup roasted, mashed butternut squash

140 g/1 cup canned chickpeas, drained and rinsed

2 heaped tablespoons tahini

juice of half a lemon

3–4 tablespoons ice cold water

salt, to taste

1 teaspoon harissa paste mixed with 1 tablespoon olive oil

SERVES 4–6

In a small frying pan/skillet, heat the olive oil, garlic and cumin over a medium heat until the garlic is sizzling and fragrant. Remove from the heat and let stand for 5 minutes.

In a food processor, combine the squash, chickpeas, tahini, lemon juice and the cooked garlic and cumin with the oil from the pan. Season with salt. Blend for 1–3 minutes, scraping down the sides with a rubber spatula. Add the ice-cold water slowly until the texture is smooth and fluffy. Drizzle with harissa oil to serve.

ZA'ATAR AND PINE NUT HUMMUS

210 g/1½ cups canned chickpeas or
  1 x 400-g/14-oz. can chickpeas,
  drained and rinsed

2 heaped tablespoons tahini

juice of half a lemon

1 small garlic clove, peeled

3–4 tablespoons ice-cold
  water

salt, to taste

25 g/¼ cup Kalamata olives, pitted
  and finely chopped

2 tablespoon pine nuts, toasted

1 tablespoon extra virgin olive oil

1 teaspoon Za'atar

SERVES 4-6

Put the chickpeas, tahini, lemon juice and garlic in a food processor. Season with salt. Blend for 1–3 minutes, scraping down the sides once or twice with a rubber spatula. Add the ice-cold water slowly until the texture is smooth and fluffy.

Top with the olives, toasted pine nuts, olive oil and za'atar to serve.

VEGETABLE-LOADED NACHOS

For such a communal food, what defines good nachos is often a very personal thing. The exact quantities for your nacho toppings will vary depending on the size of your nacho tray and your preference. The Barbecue Black Beans and Creamy Chipotle Dip make more than you'll need for these nachos, but luckily they're great in many other dishes like tacos, burritos and salads, too.

250 g/2 cups butternut squash, cut into small 1.5 cm/½-inch cubes

1 tablespoon olive or avocado oil

½ teaspoon dried and ground chipotle or cayenne pepper

tortilla chips

200 g/1 cup Barbecue Black Beans (see page 22), plus more as needed

salt, to taste

TO SERVE

115 g/½ cup guacamole (or avocado mashed with salt and pepper), plus more on the side

130 g/½ cup pico de gallo (or fresh salsa)

50 g/¼ cup Creamy Chipotle Dip (see page 29)

3 spring onions/scallions, thinly sliced

baking sheet, lined with baking parchment

SERVES 4–6

Preheat the oven to 200°C (400°F) Gas 6.

In a large bowl, toss the butternut squash cubes with the oil, ground chipotle or cayenne pepper and a sprinkling of salt to taste. Spread out evenly on a baking sheet and roast in the preheated oven for about 25 minutes until golden and tender.

Turn the oven temperature down to 180°C (350°F) Gas 4.

Spread the tortilla chips out on the lined baking sheet – enough to fill the sheet generously in a thin layer. Scatter over the roasted butternut and then the barbecue black beans, spreading them out evenly across the baking sheet. Bake in the preheated oven for about 10 minutes.

Remove from the oven and top the nachos with small dollops of guacamole or mashed avocado and pico de gallo or salsa, a drizzle of chipotle tahini sauce and a scattering of spring onions/scallions. Serve immediately either directly from the baking sheet or transfer the baking parchment onto a large plate.

NICOISE-ISH SALAD BOWL

The most delicious parts, for me, of the iconic French salad have always been the briny olives, creamy boiled potatoes and a spot-on vinaigrette. Inspired by these elements, I've created a delicious plant-based version.

150 g/¾ cup dried black or
    French/du Puy lentils, soaked
    for an hour or overnight and
    drained

1 small bunch of radishes (about
    6– 8), sliced in half lengthwise

450 g/1 lb. green beans, trimmed

225 g/8 oz. small baby potatoes

1 tablespoon avocado or olive oil

1 teaspoon fresh thyme leaves

2 teaspoons capers, drained

4 large handfuls of baby rocket/
    arugula, roughly chopped

170 g/1 cup grape tomatoes,
    chopped

¼–⅓ cup olives, pitted and
    sliced (I like to use nicoise,
    nyon or Kalamata)

salt, to taste

FOR THE DRESSING
2 teaspoons Dijon mustard

2 teaspoons apple cider vinegar

4 tablespoons olive oil

2 tablespoons very finely
    chopped shallot

salt and freshly ground black
    pepper, to taste

2 baking sheets, oiled

SERVES 2–4

First, cook the lentils in a medium saucepan with 710 ml/3 cups of water and a pinch of salt. Bring to a boil, cover with a lid and simmer for about 18–20 minutes. You want them al dente with a little bit of bite. Drain the lentils well, keeping them in the colander for at least 10 minutes to make sure they are fairly dry.

Preheat the oven to 200°C (400°F) Gas 6.

Arrange the radishes on one of the prepared baking sheets and the green beans on the other. Roast the radishes in the preheated oven for 25 minutes and the green beans for 15–20 minutes.

Meanwhile, fill a medium saucepan half full with water and bring to a boil. Add a big pinch of salt and the potatoes and boil for about 10–12 minutes until the potatoes are easily pierced with a fork. Drain and run the potatoes under cold water. When cool enough to handle, slice in half.

Heat the oil in a large frying pan/skillet over a medium-high heat. Add the cooked and drained lentils and the thyme. Season with salt and cook for 5–6 minutes, stirring only once or twice, until crispy. Stir in the capers and cook for 1 minute, then remove from the heat.

Whisk together all the dressing ingredients with 2 tablespoons of water in a bowl until combined.

Assemble the salad bowls by tossing the rocket/arugula with a spoonful or two of dressing and dividing between the bowls. Top with the green beans, potatoes, tomatoes, radishes, crispy lentils and olives. Drizzle over extra dressing to serve.

SWEET POTATO FALAFEL

These baked falafel have a soft finish and a delicate crust. Lots of great flavour comes from the fresh and ground herbs and spices, and they are easy to freeze and reheat when the mood strikes.

2 medium-sized sweet potatoes (about 350 g/12 oz.)

30 g/½ tightly packed cup coriander/cilantro

25 g/⅓ tightly packed cup flat leaf parsley leaves

2 large spring onions/green onions, roughly chopped

3 garlic cloves, peeled

1 teaspoon ground cumin

1 teaspoon ground coriander

¼ teaspoon cayenne pepper

1 teaspoon baking powder

60 g/½ cup chickpea (gram) flour

sesame seeds, to sprinkle (optional)

salt, to taste

TO SERVE
diced cucumber

diced tomato

thinly sliced red cabbage

roughly chopped flat leaf parsley

juice of ½ lemon

freshly ground black pepper

Tahini-lemon Dressing (see page 24)

pita breads

baking sheet, greased with a thin layer of olive oil

MAKES 14–16 FALAFEL
TO SERVE 4 PEOPLE

Preheat the oven to 220°C (425°F) Gas 7.

Poke the sweet potatoes with a fork a couple of times and place on the oven rack in the preheated oven. Roast for 40–60 minutes, depending on the size of your sweet potatoes, until soft. Remove from the oven and allow to cool. Once cooled, peel off and discard the skin.

Meanwhile, put the coriander/cilantro, parsley, large spring onions/green onions and garlic into a small food processor and pulse until everything is finely chopped. Alternatively, you can very finely chop these ingredients with a knife.

In a large bowl, mash the sweet potato flesh with a fork, masher or hand-held mixer until smooth. Season with salt, add the spices, baking powder and chickpea (gram) flour and stir vigorously with a rubber spatula or hand-held mixer until everything is well combined. Stir in the herb, onion and garlic mixture until evenly distributed. Let the dough rest in the fridge for 20 minutes.

Preheat the oven again to 200°C (400°F) Gas 6. Scoop out portions of dough with a spoon and then lightly roll into small balls using damp hands to prevent sticking. I go for a size that is somewhere between a ping pong ball and a golf ball. Assemble the falafel on the prepared baking sheet and sprinkle with sesame seeds, if using.

Bake in the preheated oven for 15–20 minutes until golden on the side touching the baking sheet.

To serve, combine some diced cucumber, tomato, red cabbage and parsley in a bowl with the fresh lemon juice and a little salt and pepper. Serve the falafel with the cucumber-cabbage salad and tahini-lemon dressing either in a bowl or packed into a pita bread.

ROASTED AUBERGINE/EGGPLANT PO' BOYS
with white bean purée and herby slaw

I have a deep-rooted love for New Orleans, and by 'love' I mean a strange pull to become a part of the city, learn more about it and experience it like a local. My husband and I got married there and we love planning trips back. These po' boys are my plant-based ode to New Orleans' old school charm and its new wave of creative cuisine.

FOR THE AUBERGINE/ EGGPLANT

1 large aubergine/ eggplant, sliced into 1.5-cm/½-inch thick rounds

avocado or olive oil, for brushing

1–2 tablespoons Cajun spice mix

FOR THE WHITE BEAN PURÉE

160 g/1¼ cups canned white beans, drained and rinsed

1 tablespoon tahini

1 tablespoon fresh lemon juice

½ garlic clove, peeled

¼ teaspoon chilli flakes/ hot red pepper flakes

¼ teaspoon smoked paprika

1–2 tablespoons ice-cold water (optional)

salt, to taste

FOR THE HERBY SLAW

60 g/1 cup thinly sliced red cabbage

20 g/½ tightly packed cup flat leaf parsley or coriander/cilantro leaves (or a mixture), finely chopped

½ garlic clove, finely grated

1 tablespoon olive oil

2 teaspoons apple cider vinegar

TO SERVE

fresh baguettes, cut into 15-cm/6-inch lengths and split in half

baking sheet, lined with baking parchment

MAKES 2-3 BIG
SANDWICHES OR
4 SMALLER ONES

Preheat the oven to 200°C (400°F) Gas 6.

Brush the aubergine/eggplant slices on both sides with oil and spread out on the prepared baking sheet. Sprinkle with a little of the Cajun spice mix to give a light coating.

Roast in the preheated oven for about 15 minutes. Flip the aubergine/eggplant slices over and sprinkle the other side with Cajun spice mix. Bake for another 10 minutes, until soft and golden.

To make the white bean purée, combine all the ingredients in a food processor or blender and purée until smooth. Add the ice-cold water for a smoother consistency.

Combine the slaw ingredients in a bowl and season to taste with salt.

Assemble the sandwiches with a good slathering of white bean purée on the baguettes, topped with the roasted aubergine/eggplant slices and herby slaw.

SOUPS & STEWS

As far as cosy staples go, hearty soups and stews are some of the most essential vegan recipes. They are easy to make and score extra points because most taste better the longer they sit, so they're perfect for cooking ahead. What's more comforting than a meal that's already made?

SPRING VEGETABLE SOUP

While this soup works on its own, I highly recommend serving it with a scoop of freshly made or store-bought pesto on top. It adds a herbaceous boost that matches up perfectly with thawing temperatures.

olive oil, for frying

1 onion, finely diced

2 leeks, white and light green parts only, thinly sliced into half-moons

3 garlic cloves, finely chopped

10 sprigs of fresh thyme, leaves removed from stems

1 tablespoon finely chopped fresh parsley leaves and stems

950 ml/4 cups vegetable stock/ broth

1 x 400-g/14-oz. can white beans, drained and rinsed

1 courgette/zucchini, cut into small, bite-sized pieces

125 g/1 cup frozen peas, thawed

1 carrot, peeled and shaved into ribbons

130 g/2 cups kale, stems removed and shredded

salt, to taste

Broccoli Pesto (see page 26) or store-bought vegan pesto, to serve

SERVES 4-6

Heat a thin layer of olive oil in a large saucepan or Dutch oven over a medium heat. Add the onion and leeks, season with salt and cook, stirring occasionally, for 7–8 minutes until softened.

Stir in the garlic, thyme leaves and parsley and cook for 1 minute.

Pour in the vegetable stock/broth, then turn up the heat and bring everything to a boil. Add the beans, then turn down the heat and simmer uncovered for 15 minutes, stirring a few times.

Add the courgette/zucchini and cook for another 3 minutes until the courgette/zucchini is tender but not mushy.

Stir in the peas, carrot ribbons and shredded kale and remove from the heat. Let the soup stand for about 5 minutes to let the flavours mingle.

Pour into bowls and serve with a big scoop of pesto stirred into each.

CREAMY ROASTED TOMATO SOUP

A rich and creamy tomato soup that will perk up any rainy day. Canned tomatoes actually work best for this recipe and roasting them builds an appealing sweet-and-savoury flavour. Don't be intimidated by the cashew cream, it's really simple if you have a stick blender or food processor and adds protein and a little something special to your bowl.

60 g/½ cup cashew nuts

2 x 400-g/14-oz. cans whole tomatoes

6–8 garlic cloves (depending on size), peeled and crushed with the side of a wide knife

olive oil, for frying

1 onion, finely diced

1 tablespoon tomato purée/paste

475 ml/2 cups vegetable stock/broth

salt and freshly ground black pepper, to taste

good-quality bread, for dipping

medium roasting pan, generously drizzled with olive oil

SERVES 4

Place the cashews in a container and pour over enough cold water to completely submerge. Let soak for at least 1 hour at room temperature.

Preheat the oven to 200°C (400°F) Gas 6.

Pour the canned tomatoes out onto the prepared roasting pan (with all the juices) and break apart with your hands. Be careful as they will splash your clothes – I recommend an apron or old t-shirt for this job.

Scatter the tomatoes with the garlic and season with salt. Bake in the preheated oven for 40 minutes until bubbling and the juices have slightly reduced but are still plentiful.

Meanwhile, in a large saucepan over a medium heat, warm enough olive oil to cover the base. Add the onion and cook, stirring occasionally, for about 10 minutes until softened.

Add the tomato purée/paste and cook for 2 more minutes. Pour in the vegetable stock/broth and roasted tomatoes (along with the garlic) and simmer for about 10–15 minutes. Remove from the heat.

Blend the soup with a stick blender or in batches in a food processor until smooth.

Drain the soaked cashews and blend together with a fresh 120 ml/½ cup of water with a stick blender or in a food processor until creamy.

Portion the soup into bowls and swirl in a little cashew cream to each. Serve with plenty of freshly ground black pepper and nice bread on the side for dipping.

LEEK, CAULIFLOWER AND FENNEL SOUP

Creamy, flavourful and a little on the beige side, this soup is a cosy winter favourite of mine. Roasted fennel is a very special ingredient in itself (tasting totally different from raw); it infuses this soup with mild, sweet notes. The colour of the soup can feel a little drab, so I toss in a couple of handfuls of bright green baby spinach at the very end of cooking (before blending) almost purely for cosmetic reasons.

1 head of cauliflower, cut into small florets

1 large bulb of fennel, sliced into 1.5-cm/½-inch thick pieces, long green stems and fronds cut off and set aside for garnishing

olive or avocado oil, for frying

1 leek, white and light green parts only, thinly sliced into half-moons

3 garlic cloves, finely chopped

1½ teaspoons fresh thyme leaves

950 ml/4 cups vegetable stock/broth

2 handfuls of baby spinach (optional)

salt and freshly ground black pepper, to taste

lemon wedges, to serve

good-quality bread, to serve

2 roasting pans, both greased with a thin layer of olive or avocado oil

SERVES 4

Preheat the oven to 200°C (400°F) Gas 6.

Scatter the cauliflower florets onto one of the prepared roasting pans and the sliced fennel onto the other. Season to taste with salt and roast in the preheated oven for about 20–25 minutes, until both vegetables are golden and tender.

Meanwhile, in a large saucepan, heat enough oil to cover the base over a medium heat. Add the sliced leek and a pinch of salt and cook for about 10 minutes, stirring occasionally, until softened and starting to turn golden. Stir in the garlic and cook for another minute. Add the thyme leaves and let it sizzle for 30 seconds.

Stir in the roasted cauliflower and fennel followed by the vegetable stock/broth. Turn up the heat to bring to a boil, then reduce the heat and simmer for about 5 minutes. If you're adding spinach, stir it in now and allow to wilt. Remove from the heat and allow to cool for 5 minutes.

Blend the soup with a stick blender or in batches in a food processor until smooth. Pour into bowls and serve with lemon wedges for squeezing over, ground black pepper and good bread. Garnish with the reserved fennel fronds, if you like.

GREEN THAI SOUP

This soup is perfect for using up all your green veg. It has Thai spices from green curry paste, creaminess from coconut milk, and it's packed to the brim with vegetables. You can use spinach (fresh or frozen) or Swiss chard in place of kale, or throw in that random kohlrabi that you don't know what to do with – it's all good in this soup. I prefer to serve this mostly puréed, with a helping of brown rice for texture and bulk, but you can skip the blender and keep it chunky if you prefer.

olive or avocado oil, for frying

1 leek, white and light green parts only, thinly sliced

salt, to taste

2 garlic cloves, finely chopped

2 tablespoons Thai green curry paste (check the label to make sure the brand is vegan)

1 broccoli crown with stems, chopped into small pieces

475 ml/2 cups boiling water

1 courgette/zucchini, roughly chopped

125 g/1 cup frozen peas

2 large handfuls of kale, stems removed and roughly chopped

1 x 400-g/14-oz. can coconut milk (I use full fat)

5 sprigs of fresh coriander/cilantro with stems (plus more for serving), roughly chopped

cooked brown rice, to serve (optional)

SERVES 3–4

In a large saucepan with a lid, heat a good glug of oil over a medium-high heat. Add the leek, season to taste with salt and cook, stirring occasionally, for about 5–7 minutes, until the leek has softened.

Add the garlic and fry for another minute. Stir in the curry paste and cook for another minute. Add the broccoli and boiling water to the pan and stir.

Bring to a simmer and add the courgette/zucchini. Cover the pan and simmer for about 5 minutes until the vegetables are tender.

Stir in the peas and kale, cover, and cook for another 1–2 minutes until the kale has wilted. Turn off the heat and stir in coconut milk (reserving a little to garnish) and coriander/cilantro.

If blending, use a stick blender or purée in batches in a food processor until mostly smooth.

Served the soup in bowls with extra coriander/cilantro, a drizzle of the reserved coconut milk and a portion of cooked brown rice, if desired.

GINGER COCONUT BROTH with veggies and noodles

This falls somewhere between a soup, a curry and a brothy ramen bowl. With ginger, chilli and garlic flavours it often hits the spot when I'm looking for something that I can slurp a big bowl of without it weighing me down.

FOR THE BROTH

2 teaspoons avocado oil

4 garlic cloves, finely chopped or grated

2 tablespoons grated fresh ginger

1 x 400-g/14-oz. can coconut milk (I use full fat)

2 tablespoons tamari

120 ml/½ cup water or vegetable stock/broth

¼ teaspoon chilli flakes/hot red pepper flakes (optional)

ADD-INS

120-170 g/4-6 oz. soba noodles

1 courgette/zucchini, peeled or spiralized into noodles or cut into julienne

1 carrot, spiralized into noodles or cut into julienne

130 g/1 cup shelled frozen edamame beans, thawed

SERVES 2–3

Cook the soba noodles in boiling water according to the package instructions. (The 100% buckwheat soba noodles I use usually take about 8 minutes.)

While the soba noodles are cooking, heat the avocado oil in a large saucepan or high-sided frying pan/skillet over a medium-high heat. Add the garlic and ginger and let them sizzle for about 30–60 seconds until fragrant, but not browning.

Add the coconut milk and tamari and stir. Add the water or vegetable stock/broth and chilli flakes/hot red pepper flakes (if using).

Bring to a simmer, then stir in the courgette/zucchini, carrot and edamame beans and let everything warm through for about 2 minutes. Remove from heat.

Divide the cooked soba noodles between bowls and pour the hot broth and veggies over to serve.

PUMPKIN COCONUT SOUP with warming spices

This spiced soup is a great warmer for the first chilly weeks of fall/autumn. With its slight sweetness, bold spice combination and nutty grains to serve, it feels grounding and cosy while setting itself apart from other plain pumpkin soups. I've even eaten it for breakfast because it can kind of feel like an exotic porridge. It's really nice served with some fresh coriander/cilantro leaves and a squeeze of fresh lime juice.

1 tablespoon avocado or coconut oil

1 onion, diced

3 garlic cloves, finely chopped

2 tablespoons grated fresh ginger

1 teaspoon ground cumin

½ teaspoon ground cinnamon

½ teaspoon cayenne pepper

¼ teaspoon ground nutmeg

pinch of ground allspice

2 carrots, roughly chopped

450 g/3½ cups diced pumpkin or 2 x 400-g/14-oz. cans pumpkin or butternut squash purée

475 ml/2 cups boiling water

1 x 400-g/14-oz. can coconut milk (I use full fat)

salt, to taste

135 g/1 cup cooked brown rice, barley or farro, to serve

SERVES 4–6

In a large saucepan with a lid, heat the oil over a medium heat. Add the onion, season with salt and cook, stirring occasionally, for about 6–8 minutes, until the onion is turning golden.

Add the garlic, ginger, cumin, cinnamon, cayenne pepper, nutmeg and allspice and cook for 1 minute, stirring everything frequently.

Add the carrots and pumpkin and season with salt. Pour in the boiling water and stir. Cover and cook for about 10 minutes. Remove the lid and simmer for another 10 minutes, until the vegetables are tender.

Turn off the heat and stir in the coconut milk. Blend with a stick blender or in batches in a food processor until smooth. Divide the soup into bowls and serve with a scoop of cooked brown rice, barley or farro in each.

BUTTERNUT SQUASH AND BLACK BEAN CHILLI

Cubes of butternut squash and black beans make this chilli hearty and satisfying. I'll make this on a Sunday afternoon to eat throughout the week. The flavours deepen when it has time to sit, so it tastes even better the second or third time around.

avocado or olive oil, for frying

1 onion, diced

375 g/3 cups peeled butternut squash, cut into small 1.5-cm/½-inch cubes

2 tablespoons tomato purée/paste

1 large garlic clove, finely chopped

3 teaspoons ground cumin

2 teaspoons smoked paprika

¼ teaspoon ground cinnamon

¼ teaspoon cayenne pepper

1 x 400-g/14-oz. can crushed or chopped tomatoes in juices

2 x 400-g/14-oz. cans black beans in their liquid (I use the low sodium version)

salt, to taste

TO SERVE (OPTIONAL)
diced avocado or Basic Avocado Dip (see page 29)

vegan sour cream

chopped large spring onions/green onions

corn chips

SERVES 4–6

In a large saucepan with a lid, heat enough oil to cover the base of the pan over a medium heat.

Add the onion, season with salt and cook for about 5 minutes until translucent. Add the butternut squash and cook, stirring occasionally, for 5 minutes.

Add the tomato purée/paste and stir. Cook for 1 minute. Add the garlic, cumin, paprika, cinnamon and cayenne pepper and cook for 1 minute more. Pour in the tomatoes and black beans along with the liquid from the cans. Season with salt and reduce the heat to medium-low.

Cook covered for about 30 minutes, stirring occasionally, until the butternut is tender. You may need to add 120 ml/½ cup or more water, if the chilli becomes too dry or thick for your liking. Serve with your desired toppings.

MOROCCAN-SPICED LENTIL STEW

This richly spiced tomato-based stew is easy enough to put together on a weeknight and leftovers make a great lunch the next day. I like serving this with warm pita breads.

FOR THE LENTILS

160 g/¾ cup dried black or French/du Puy lentils, soaked for an hour or overnight and drained

FOR THE STEW

olive oil, for frying

1 small red onion, finely diced

1 yellow (bell) pepper, deseeded and finely diced

2 tablespoons tomato purée/ paste

2 teaspoons sweet smoked paprika

1 teaspoon ground cumin

½ teaspoon ground coriander

2 garlic cloves, finely chopped

2 x 400-g/14-oz. cans crushed or chopped tomatoes in juice

pinch of saffron threads (optional)

1 large handful of fresh baby spinach, roughly chopped

1 tablespoon harissa

1 tablespoon agave syrup

salt, to taste

freshly chopped parsley or coriander/cilantro, to serve

toasted bread, flatbread or pita breads, to serve

SERVES 4–5

Put the lentils in a medium saucepan with 710 ml/3 cups of water and a pinch of salt. Bring to a boil, then reduce the heat to medium-low, cover with a lid and cook for about 18–20 minutes. You want them al dente with a little bit of bite. When cooked, drain the lentils in a colander.

Meanwhile, heat a thin layer of oil in a large frying pan/skillet with high sides and a lid or in a Dutch oven over a medium heat. Add the onion and (bell) pepper, season with salt and sauté for 4–6 minutes until the onion is translucent.

Stir in the tomato purée/paste and cook for 1 minute. Add the spices and garlic and cook for 30 seconds more. Stir in the tomatoes and saffron (if using). Cover with a lid and simmer over a medium-low heat for 15 minutes.

Add the cooked and drained lentils to the tomato mixture and cook, uncovered, for another 10 minutes, until the liquid has slightly reduced.

Stir in the spinach and let it wilt. Remove from the heat and stir in the harissa and agave syrup. Serve warm scattered with freshly chopped herbs and pita bread to mop up the sauce.

SWEET POTATO AND WHITE BEAN STEW

White beans lend a creaminess to this stew which, when combined with sweet potato, sage and rosemary, feels like the food version of a cosy sweater. I'm all for canned beans – especially in a pinch – but I really notice a better quality when I cook my own white beans from dried. That said, you can definitely make this stew with canned white beans, so skip step one in the method below if you do.

170 g/1 cup dried white beans (or 270 g/2 cups cooked white beans)

a few sprigs of mixed fresh herbs (optional)

1 tablespoon olive oil

1 onion, finely diced

3 garlic cloves, finely chopped

1 large sweet potato, peeled and cut into 1.5-cm/½-inch cubes

2 carrots, diced

1 tablespoon freshly chopped rosemary leaves

3 freshly chopped sage leaves

950 ml/4 cups vegetable stock/broth

sea salt and freshly ground black pepper, to taste

roughly chopped fresh parsley, to garnish

SERVES 4–5

If using dried white beans, soak them overnight in cold water for at least 8 hours or longer. When you're ready to cook them, drain off the soaking liquid and discard, then put the beans in a medium saucepan and cover with fresh water.

Bring to a boil, adding a pinch of salt and any fresh herbs you have lying around (a few thyme sprigs, sage leaves, parsley stems, etc.). Simmer for about 30–40 minutes, or until tender. The cooking time will depend on your beans, how long they were soaked for and how old they are. Drain the beans and set aside.

In a large saucepan, heat the olive oil over a medium heat. Add the onion and cook, stirring occasionally, for about 5 minutes, until softened. Add the garlic and cook for 1 minute more. Stir in the sweet potato, carrots, rosemary and sage. Season well with salt and cook for another 2–3 minutes until the herbs are fragrant.

Add the cooked and drained white beans and the vegetable stock/broth and bring everything to a boil. Simmer over a medium-low heat, covered with a lid for 20 minutes until the sweet potato has softened. Uncover, stir and simmer for a final 5 minutes. Crush a few white beans against the side of the pot with a wooden spoon to release their starch and thicken the stew. Spoon the stew into bowls and garnish with chopped parsley and freshly ground black pepper to serve.

BIG BOWLS
& MAIN MEALS

Big bowls of plant-based goodness containing grains, veggies, legumes, flavourful sauces and more are what I eat most often for lunch and mid-week dinner. Other meals in this chapter, such as paella, burgers and curry are great staples for weekend dining or entertaining.

MEZZE BOWL

Lots of texture, flavours and freshness make this recipe one you'll want to share. Any of the tahini dressings from the basics chapter would be nice here, or serve with Garlic Greens and Hummus, along with a side of pita.

5–7 carrots, sliced diagonally into ovals

1 tablespoon olive oil, plus extra to serve

1 teaspoon apple cider vinegar

1 teaspoon ground cumin

85 g/½ cup dried quinoa

large handful of freshly chopped mint leaves

large handful of freshly chopped parsley

seeds from ½ pomegranate

¼ cucumber, cut into small pieces

freshly squeezed juice of half a lemon

salt

OPTIONAL TOPPINGS
Garlic Greens (see page 33)

warm pita

Garlic Yogurt Dip (see page 29)

Hummus (see page 144)

Tahini-harissa Dressing (see page 25)

SERVES 2–3

Preheat the oven to 200°C (400°F) Gas 6.

Toss the carrots with the olive oil, vinegar, cumin and a pinch of salt. Spread out in a roasting pan and roast in the preheated oven for about 30 minutes (rotating the pan at the 15 minute mark).

Meanwhile, in a small saucepan, combine the quinoa with 235 ml/1 cup of water. Bring to a boil, add a pinch of salt and reduce to a simmer. Cover with a lid and simmer for about 15 minutes, or until all the liquid is absorbed. Remove from the heat and keep covered for about 10 minutes. Fluff with a fork and allow to cool.

In a bowl, combine the cooled quinoa with the chopped herbs, pomegranate seeds, cucumber, lemon juice and a drizzle of oil and toss to mix.

Divide the quinoa into bowls. Add the roasted carrots and any extra toppings you like.

GREEN KITCHARI BOWL

Kitchari is a very simple combination of lentils or split peas, rice and spices – but the result is something wholesome and deeply comforting, kind of like an Indian-spiced risotto. Originating in South Asia, in the traditional healing concept of ayurveda, it's often used as a cleansing meal to healthily balance the three bodily doshas.

180 g/1 cup dried yellow split peas or lentils

90 g/½ cup long grain brown or jasmine rice

2–3 tablespoons coconut oil

1 tablespoon grated fresh ginger

2 teaspoons ground cumin

1 teaspoon ground coriander

1 teaspoon fennel seeds

1 teaspoon ground fenugreek

1 teaspoon ground turmeric

1.2 litres/5 cups water or vegetable stock/broth

1 crown broccoli, cut up very small into an almost rice-like texture

1 medium courgette/ zucchini, trimmed and coarsely grated

60 g/1 packed cup baby spinach or baby kale, roughly chopped

salt, to taste

freshly chopped coriander/ cilantro, to serve

Garlic Yogurt Dip (see page 29), to serve (optional)

SERVES 4–6

Rinse the yellow split peas or lentils and rice in a colander under cold water until the water runs clear.

In a large saucepan over a medium-high heat, heat enough coconut oil to cover the base of the pan. Add the ginger and cook, stirring, for 30 seconds. Add the spices, season with salt and cook for another 30 seconds, until fragrant.

Add the lentils and rice and stir to coat in the spices. Pour in the water or vegetable stock/broth and bring to a boil.

Reduce the heat to medium-low, cover with a lid and simmer for 35–45 minutes, stirring occasionally until the rice and lentils are tender but not mushy and most of the liquid has been absorbed. (You may need to add a little more liquid if the mixture becomes too dry.)

Stir in the broccoli. Cover and cook for another 4–5 minutes. Stir in the courgette/zucchini and spinach or kale, then remove from the heat and leave to stand for 5 minutes. Serve warm scattered with freshly chopped coriander/cilantro and garlic yogurt dip, if desired.

WINTER VEGETABLE BOWL

Winter can be rough on us veggie lovers, when farm fresh tomatoes and juicy stone fruit seem another world away. Here's a bowl that celebrates cold weather produce and perks it up with a tasty lemon and olive chermoula and crunchy toasted walnuts.

130 g/¾ cup wild rice

1 acorn squash, sliced in half and seeds removed, then sliced into thin half-moons

1 red onion, cut into 1.5-cm/ ½-inch wedges

1–2 tablespoons avocado or olive oil

300 g/3 cups Brussels sprouts, woody bases and outer leaves removed, then thinly sliced (so you get ribbons of Brussels sprouts leaves)

2 big handfuls of baby rocket/ arugula or spinach

salt and freshly ground black pepper, to taste

Chermoula (see page 26), to serve

50 g/⅓ cup toasted walnuts, roughly chopped, to serve

a roasting pan, oiled

SERVES 3–4

Preheat the oven to 220°C (425°F) Gas 7.

In a medium saucepan, combine the wild rice with 350 ml/1½ cups of water. Cover with a lid and bring to a boil. Add a pinch of salt, reduce the heat to medium-low and simmer for about 40 minutes, or according to the package instructions, until the rice is cooked.

Meanwhile, arrange the squash and onion in the prepared roasting pan. Roast in the preheated oven for about 25–30 minutes, rotating the pan and flipping the veg half-way through.

Meanwhile, heat the oil in a large saucepan or a frying pan/skillet with high sides over a medium-high heat. Add the shredded Brussels sprouts and sprinkle with a good pinch of salt. Cook, stirring a few times, for about 5 minutes until the sprouts are softened; they should be mostly bright green but golden in places. Stir in the rocket/arugula or spinach and remove from the heat. Taste and add salt and pepper as desired.

To assemble the bowls, start with a scoop of rice and top with lots of Brussels sprouts, roasted squash and red onion. Add a generous drizzle of chermoula and walnuts to finish.

COCONUT BROWN RICE BOWL
with jerk spice roasted vegetables

Warming jerk spices, creamy coconut rice and bright lime juice make for a low-key tropical bowl for all seasons. You can swap the courgette/zucchini and asparagus for other vegetables (though roasting times will vary).

FOR THE COCONUT BROWN RICE

100 g/½ cup brown rice

75 ml/⅓ cup coconut milk

pinch of salt

FOR THE JERK SPICE MIX [MAKES ABOUT 25 G/¼ CUP]

1 teaspoon ground allspice

1 teaspoon curry powder

1 teaspoon onion powder

½ teaspoon garlic powder

½ teaspoon cayenne pepper

¼ teaspoon ground ginger

¼ teaspoon ground nutmeg

¼ teaspoon freshly ground black pepper

1 teaspoon salt

FOR THE VEGETABLES

2 courgettes/zucchini or yellow summer squash, cut diagonally into 1.5-cm/½-inch thick ovals

1–2 tablespoons olive oil

1 bunch of asparagus, woody ends snapped off and cut into bite-sized pieces

salt and freshly ground black pepper

TO SERVE

1 spring onion/scallion, finely chopped

1 avocado, peeled, pitted and cut into bite-sized pieces

toasted pumpkin seeds/pepitas or Crispy Chickpeas (see page 21)

lime wedges

SERVES 2–3

Combine the rice, coconut milk and 235 ml/1 cup of water in a saucepan over a medium-high heat. Cover with a lid and bring to a boil. Add the salt, then reduce the heat to medium-low and simmer, covered, for about 40–45 minutes until the rice is cooked and creamy and the liquid has been absorbed.

Meanwhile, combine all the jerk spice mix ingredients in a small jar with a lid and shake until blended together.

Preheat the oven to 200°C (400°F) Gas 6.

In a large bowl, mix together the courgettes/zucchini with enough olive oil to coat and about 2 teaspoons of the jerk spice mix. Toss well to coat the courgettes/zucchini in the spice. Spread the courgettes/zucchini out in a roasting pan, being careful not to crowd them. Repeat by tossing the asparagus in the oil and jerk spice mix and spread out on a separate roasting pan.

Roast the vegetables in the preheated oven for about 15–20 minutes, turning halfway through, until golden. Taste and adjust the seasoning with salt and pepper, if needed.

Assemble the bowls starting with a portion of coconut rice, then the roasted spiced vegetables, spring onion/scallion, avocado and toasted pumpkin seeds/pepitas or crispy chickpeas. Serve with lime wedges for squeezing over.

SOY AND GINGER DELICATA SQUASH BOWL

Delicata squash is kind of the best— it looks fancy, you don't have to peel it and it has a subtle nuttiness that goes well with so many different flavours. I recommend roasting a big batch ahead of time and using some in this dish. If you can't get your hands on delicata, you can use whatever roasted vegetables are more readily available to you (broccoli, butternut or peppers would all be nice). Serve with a drizzle of sriracha or chilli paste for a spicier bowl.

1 delicata squash, cut in half lengthwise, deseeded and sliced into half-moons

175 g/6 oz. soba noodles

1 tablespoon olive or avocado oil

2.5-cm/1-inch piece of fresh ginger, finely grated

2 garlic cloves, finely chopped

50 g/2 cups kale, stems removed and shredded

3 tablespoons tamari or soy sauce

1 tablespoon pure maple syrup

2 large spring onions/green onions, thinly sliced, to serve

toasted sesame seeds, to serve (optional)

roasting pan, oiled

SERVES 2-3

Preheat the oven to 220°C (425°F) Gas 7.

Arrange the squash in the prepared roasting pan so that each piece has plenty of room. Roast in the preheated oven for 20–25 minutes, until golden, flipping with a spatula halfway through.

Meanwhile, cook the soba noodles in boiling water following the package instructions (I cook mine for 6 minutes, but the cooking time will vary according to the type of noodle). Drain and rinse under cold water while in the colander.

In a large frying pan/skillet, heat the oil over a medium-high heat. Add the ginger and garlic and cook, stirring, for 1 minute. Add the kale and cook for about 2–3 minutes until wilted.

Add the tamari or soy and maple syrup and stir vigorously to combine. Add the noodles and squash and stir gently to coat everything.

Portion into bowls and serve with large spring onions/green onions and toasted sesame seeds.

STIR FRY BOWL

Some weeknights require a good stir-fry to end things on a simple but satisfying note. If you made a batch of Spicy Tofu (see page 21) in advance, this is where you can put leftovers to good use.

100 g/½ cup brown rice (I also like a mixture of wild and brown rice)

pinch of salt

1 tablespoon peeled and very finely chopped fresh ginger

2 garlic cloves, very finely chopped

4 large spring onions/green onions, thinly sliced

1 bunch of baby broccoli, broccolini or regular broccoli (about 120 g/2 cups), cut into bite-sized pieces

200 g/2 cups mangetout/snow peas

avocado oil, for frying

1 teaspoon rice vinegar

2 tablespoons tamari

½ portion of Spicy Tofu (see page 21)

sesame seeds, to garnish (optional)

SERVES 2

Combine the rice and 235 ml/1 cup of water in a saucepan over a medium-high heat. Cover with a lid and bring to a boil. Add the pinch of salt, then reduce the heat to medium-low and simmer, covered, for about 35–40 minutes until the rice is tender and the water has been absorbed.

Towards the end of the rice cooking time, mix the ginger, garlic and large spring onions/green onions together in a small bowl. Combine the broccoli and mangetout/snow peas on a plate, ready for frying. Depending on the size of your pan, you may need to divide all the ingredients (including the oil, vinegar and tamari) in half and fry in two batches to avoid overcrowding.

In a large wok or frying pan/skillet, heat a thin layer of oil over a high heat. Add the onion mixture and cook for 5 seconds. Toss in the broccoli and mangetout/snow peas and stir fry for about 5–6 minutes until seared and golden. If you need to re-heat the spicy tofu, add this now to warm through. Add the rice vinegar and tamari and stir fry for 30–60 seconds. Remove from the pan and transfer to a plate. Repeat the process with the remaining ingredients if needed.

Drain and then divide the hot cooked rice into bowls. Pile the vegetables and spicy tofu on top and serve with a sprinkling of sesame seeds to garnish, if you like.

ITALIAN POLENTA

This recipe doubles as a savoury breakfast or easy weeknight dinner. You can make your own pesto if you have the time and plenty of basil (see recipe on page 26) or just use a vegan store-bought brand.

350 g/12 oz. cherry or grape tomatoes

2 tablespoons olive oil

1.2 litres/4–5 cups water or stock of choice

150 g/1 cup fine polenta/cornmeal (the fine grind makes it cook very quickly!)

2 tablespoons finely grated vegan hard cheese, plus extra to serve

sea salt and freshly ground black pepper, to taste

OPTIONAL TOPPINGS
4 tablespoons Broccoli Pesto (see page 26)

garlic chives (optional)

baking sheet lined with baking parchment

SERVES 4

Preheat the oven to 190°C (375°F) Gas 5.

Spread the tomatoes over the lined baking sheet, sprinkle with a little salt and roast in the preheated oven for 15–20 minutes until collapsing and lightly browned in places. When you remove them from the oven, drizzle with 1 tablespoon of the olive oil and toss to coat. Taste for seasoning and set aside.

Meanwhile, in a large saucepan, bring the water or stock to a boil (if using water, you can boil it in the kettle first to save time). Once it's at a rolling boil, stir in the polenta/cornmeal with a wooden spoon, then reduce to a simmer.

Season with a good amount of salt (I usually use around 1 teaspoon, depending on the liquid I'm using). Cook, uncovered, stirring regularly, until the liquid is absorbed. For finely ground polenta, this can take as little as 1 minute, or up to 10 minutes. Cover and leave to stand until you're ready to serve. Note: If you've let it sit for a little while, you may need to gently reheat and add a little more liquid to get it to your desired consistency. Stir in the remaining tablespoon of olive oil, the vegan hard cheese and a few grinds of black pepper.

Portion into bowls and top with a spoonful of pesto, roasted tomatoes, garlic chives (if using) and extra grated vegan hard cheese.

QUINOA AND RED LENTIL RISOTTO
with asparagus and peas

The pairing of red lentils and quinoa is perfect for a plant-based protein-packed risotto. The lentils cook quickly and lose their shape, adding to the creaminess of the dish, while quinoa provides a pleasantly nutty flavour and bite. Quick and low-maintenance, this is also a cheat's risotto with less ladling and stirring than traditional versions.

RISOTTO

90 g/½ cup dried red lentils, soaked, then drained and rinsed

85 g/½ cup quinoa, soaked, then drained and rinsed

875 ml/3½ cups vegetable stock

2 tablespoons finely grated vegan hard cheese (optional), plus extra to serve

ASPARAGUS AND PEAS

½ bunch asparagus (about 225 g/ 8 oz.), woody ends trimmed and cut into 2.5-cm/1-inch pieces

1 garlic clove, finely chopped

75 g/½ cup frozen peas, thawed

squeeze of fresh lemon juice

salt and freshly ground black pepper

olive oil, for frying

SERVES 2

Combine the lentils, quinoa, stock and salt to taste in a medium saucepan. Cover and bring to the boil over a medium-high heat. Reduce to a simmer and cook, covered, for 15 minutes, stirring occasionally. Remove the lid and cook for another 3–5 minutes. Take off the heat when most of the liquid has been absorbed, the red lentils have broken down, and the texture is creamy. Stir in the vegan hard cheese (if using), then taste for seasoning.

Meanwhile, heat a frying pan/skillet over a medium heat. Add enough olive oil to cover the base of the pan in a thin layer and heat through for 30 seconds–1 minute. Add the asparagus, sprinkle with a generous pinch of salt and cook, stirring once or twice, for 4–5 minutes until the asparagus is browning in spots but still bright green. Add the garlic and 2 or 3 tablespoons of water if the pan is dry, and toss to combine. Cover and cook for another 1 minute. Remove the lid and stir in the peas, then remove from the heat and adjust the seasoning with salt and pepper. Add the lemon juice just before serving.

Serve the risotto topped with the asparagus and peas and more grated vegan hard cheese, if desired.

CHICKPEA 'TIKKA' MASALA

The Indian takeout staple gets a vegan makeover with chickpeas in a lush tomato-based sauce. Serve with fluffy rice, chopped chilli/chile, fresh herbs and naan breads on the side for a simple and satisfying feast.

coconut oil, for frying

1 onion, finely diced

1 yellow (bell) pepper, deseeded and finely chopped

2 garlic cloves, finely chopped

2 teaspoons garam masala

1 teaspoon ground cumin

½ teaspoon ground turmeric

2 carrots, peeled and finely chopped

2 x 400-g/14-oz. cans of chickpeas, drained and rinsed

2 x 400-g/14-oz. cans of finely chopped tomatoes in juice or crushed tomatoes

1 x-400-g/14-oz. can coconut milk (I use full fat)

¼ teaspoon cayenne pepper (optional)

salt, to taste

TO SERVE [OPTIONAL]
cooked brown rice or quinoa

naan breads

freshly chopped coriander/ cilantro leaves

freshly chopped chilli/chile

SERVES 6

Heat enough coconut oil to generously coat the bottom of a large saucepan over a medium-high heat.

Add the onion and (bell) pepper and season with salt. Cook, stirring, for about 10 minutes.

Add the garlic and cook for 1 minute. Add the garam masala, cumin and turmeric and cook for another 30 seconds, until fragrant.

Add the carrots, chickpeas and tomatoes. Bring to a boil, then reduce to a simmer and cover with a lid. Simmer for about 15–20 minutes.

Stir in the coconut milk, then simmer for 5 minutes more and remove from the heat. Stir in the cayenne pepper, if using. Let the curry stand, covered with a lid to keep warm, for at least 15 minutes to let the flavours mingle.

Serve over brown rice or quinoa, with naan breads, fresh herbs and chilli/chile, as desired.

RED LENTIL DAHL

This is a perfect store cupboard meal. A combination of lentils, canned tomatoes and a bunch of spices from your arsenal, this is the type of comforting stew you can throw together on a cold afternoon or evening when you really can't be bothered to leave the house.

olive oil or coconut oil,
   for frying

2 onions, finely sliced

3 garlic cloves, finely chopped

2.5-cm/1-inch piece of fresh
   ginger, grated

2 teaspoons ground cumin

1 teaspoon ground turmeric

1 teaspoon ground coriander

½ teaspoon garam masala

¼ teaspoon cayenne pepper

1 x 400-g/14-oz. can chopped
   tomatoes

270 g/1½ cups dried red lentils

2 carrots, finely diced

120 g/2 cups kale, shredded

salt and freshly ground black
   pepper, to taste

TO SERVE
steamed rice

pinch of chilli flakes/hot red
   pepper flakes

freshly chopped coriander/
   cilantro

coconut cream

SERVES 4-6

Heat enough oil to thinly coat the base of a large saucepan over a medium-high heat. Add the onions, season to taste with salt and cook for about 10–12 minutes, stirring occasionally, until they begin to caramelize. Add a splash of water if the pan gets too dry.

Add the garlic and ginger and cook for another minute. Stir in the spices and cook for 1 more minute. Add the tomatoes and cook until bubbling again, then add 950 ml/4 cups of water and the lentils. Cover with a lid and bring to a boil.

Add the carrots, cover, and simmer for about 20–30 minutes until the lentils are starting to break down and the carrots are tender. Stir in some black pepper and the kale.

Turn off the heat, leave the pan covered and allow to stand for 15 minutes before serving with rice, chilli flakes/hot red pepper flakes, coriander/cilantro and a drizzle of coconut cream.

VEGETABLE PAELLA

This veggie version of paella has an authentic flavour base which comes from golden saffron, tomatoes, piquillo peppers and smoked paprika.

FOR THE MUSHROOM VEGETABLE BROTH

950 ml/4 cups vegetable stock/broth

10 g/⅓ cup mixed dried mushrooms

5 garlic cloves, skins left on and crushed with the side of a wide knife

FOR THE BASE

1 medium onion, roughly chopped

3 garlic cloves, peeled

1 medium tomato, quartered

2 roasted piquillo red peppers from a jar, drained

2 tablespoons olive oil

1 teaspoon apple cider vinegar

1 teaspoon smoked paprika (I used sweet but spicy is good too)

salt, to taste

FOR THE VEGETABLES

olive oil, for frying

225 g/8 oz. mixed mushrooms (cremini, portobello, oyster are all good here), sliced

1 fennel bulb, thinly sliced lengthwise

1 small or ½ large red (bell) pepper, deseeded and cut into strips

1 small or ½ large yellow (bell) pepper, deseeded and cut into strips

100 g/¾ cup frozen peas, thawed

FOR THE RICE

2 tablespoons olive oil

240 g/1¼ heaped cups Arborio rice

generous pinch of saffron threads

SERVES 4

For the broth, pour the vegetable stock/broth into a saucepan with the dried mushrooms and garlic. Cover and bring to a boil. Simmer, covered, for 15–20 minutes, then remove from the heat and let stand until needed. When ready to use the stock/broth, remove and discard the mushrooms and garlic and gently reheat.

Meanwhile, pulse the base ingredients in a food processor until finely chopped but not puréed.

For the vegetables, heat about 2 tablespoons oil in a paella pan or large frying pan/skillet with high sides. Add the mushrooms and season with salt. Cook over a medium heat for about 3–5 minutes, until tender and golden. Set aside.

Add a little more oil, the fennel and (bell) peppers and season with salt. Cook, stirring a few times, until caramelized and tender (about 5–7 minutes). Remove from the pan and set aside on a plate.

For the rice, heat the olive oil over a medium heat in the same pan. Add the rice and cook for 1–2 minutes, stirring, until the rice is coated in oil and almost translucent. Stir in the tomato-onion base and cook for 2 minutes. Add the mushroom and vegetable stock/broth and the saffron. Make sure the rice is in an even layer across the pan.

Turn the heat up to medium-high and cook for 20–25 minutes, uncovered, without stirring, until the rice is al dente. You should hear a slight popping sound towards the end, which means a delicious crisp crust is forming at the bottom.

Place the cooked vegetables (including peas) on top of the cooked rice, turn off the heat and cover the pan with a clean kitchen cloth. Let stand for 5 minutes. Serve warm straight from the pan.

BLACK BEAN AND BEET BURGERS

No longer considered an afterthought, veggie burgers have become a main attraction at many trendy eateries. I find this smoky and substantial plant-based patty works well with lots of different toppings.

olive oil, for frying

1 small red onion, finely diced

2 garlic cloves, finely chopped

2 tablespoons flax seeds

50 g/½ cup rolled oats

2 x 400-g/14-oz. cans black beans, drained and rinsed

2 medium beetroot/beets, grated

2 tablespoons tomato purée/paste

1½ teaspoons smoked paprika

1 teaspoon dried oregano

salt and freshly ground black pepper, to taste

OPTIONAL SERVING SUGGESTIONS

toasted English muffins or buns

barbecue sauce

smashed avocado

Caramelized Onions (see page 30)

sliced tomato

rocket/arugula or lettuce

MAKES 6–8 PATTIES

Heat a thin layer of olive oil in a medium frying pan/skillet over a medium heat. Add the onion and cook, stirring, for about 5 minutes until softened. Add the garlic and cook for 1 minute more. Remove from the heat and set aside.

In a large bowl, combine the flax seeds with 6 tablespoons water and let stand for 10 minutes.

Meanwhile, in a food processor, process the oats until they are finely chopped and bordering on a flour-like texture. Add the black beans to the food processor and pulse until they're finely chopped and combined with the oats, but not puréed.

Put the processed oats and black beans, grated beetroot/beets, cooked onions and garlic, tomato purée/paste, smoked paprika and oregano into the large bowl with the flax seeds. Season with salt and pepper and mix with a rubber spatula or with your hands until everything is well combined. Form the mixture into 6–8 patties using damp hands, making them about 2.5 cm/1 inch thick and about 7.5 cm/3 inches wide.

In a large frying pan/skillet, heat enough oil to cover the base over a medium-high heat. Add two patties and cook for 3–4 minutes on one side, until browned and firm. Flip and cook for another 3–4 minutes on the other side. Reduce the heat to medium if the patties are getting too charred. Remove and repeat with the remaining burgers.

Alternatively, you can lightly brush the burgers with oil and bake them on a baking sheet lined with parchment paper for 25 minutes in an oven preheated to 200°C (400°F) Gas 6, flipping them halfway through the cooking time.

Serve warm on toasted English muffins or buns with plenty of your chosen toppings.

MUSHROOM AND LENTIL NO-MEAT-BALLS

These no-meatballs aren't pretending to be something they're not; rather, they taste like the umami-rich mushrooms, herbs, spices and earthy lentils that they're made from. They're great with both tomato sauce and pesto, as well as in salads, pasta and served as these delicious meatball sliders.

170 g/1 cup dried green lentils

700–900 ml/3–4 cups water or vegetable stock/broth

olive oil, for frying

1 red onion, finely diced

3 garlic cloves, finely chopped

1 teaspoon dried oregano

¼ teaspoon fennel seeds

2 tablespoons ground chia seeds

140 g/2 cups of mushrooms (baby portabello or cremini work great for this), roughly chopped

50 g/⅓ cup raw walnuts, roughly chopped

1 tablespoon tomato purée/paste

2 tablespoons oat flour

salt, to taste

TO SERVE (OPTIONAL)
seeded rolls

Broccoli Pesto (see page 26)

tomato sauce

rocket/arugula

baking sheet, lined with baking parchment

MAKES 12–14

In a large saucepan, combine the lentils with the water or vegetable stock/broth (enough to generously cover the lentils). Add a pinch of salt and bring to a boil. Reduce the heat and simmer over a medium-low heat for 20–25 minutes until tender but not mushy. Once cooked, drain.

In a large frying pan/skillet, heat enough olive oil to cover the base of the pan over a medium-high heat. Cook the onion for 4–5 minutes, stirring occasionally, until softened and translucent. Add the garlic, oregano and fennel seeds and season with salt. Cook for another minute until fragrant.

Meanwhile, combine the ground chia seeds with 6 tablespoons of water in a small bowl and leave to stand for at least 5 minutes.

In a food processor or blender, combine the cooked lentils, mushrooms, cooked onion mixture, walnuts, tomato purée/paste, chia seeds and oat flour. Process to a rough, slightly chunky dough, scraping down the sides a couple of times.

Preheat the oven to 180°C (350°F) Gas 4.

Form the mixture into golf ball-sized balls and arrange close together on the prepared baking sheet. Bake in the preheated oven for 30 minutes until slightly browned and warmed through. Great served as sliders in rolls with pesto, tomato sauce and rocket/arugula, if desired.

BAKES & DESSERTS

Ending on a sweet note is how I prefer to roll.
I think if you want dessert every day, you should
have it. These treats focus on fruits, alternative
flours, nuts and seeds for a plant-centric twist.
Most are so naturally full of the good stuff that
they are suitable for breakfast as well as dessert.

CHICKPEA AND CHOCOLATE CHIP COOKIES

These chewy and chocolatey cookies are the dessert I always want on-hand. They get their great texture from coconut oil, have just the right amount of sweetness, and use protein-rich chickpea (gram) flour, which leaves me feeling truly satisfied.

2 tablespoons ground chia seeds

120 ml/½ cup gently melted coconut oil

100 g/½ cup coconut sugar or soft light brown sugar

1 teaspoon vanilla extract

185 g/1½ cups chickpea (gram) flour

1 teaspoon baking powder

¼ teaspoon salt

50 g/⅓ cup dark/bittersweet vegan chocolate chips or roughly chopped chocolate

flaky sea salt, for sprinkling on top (optional)

baking sheet, lined with baking parchment

MAKES ABOUT 12

In a large bowl, combine the ground chia seeds with 6 tablespoons of water and whisk to combine; this should form a gel-like consistency.

Add the melted coconut oil to the bowl with the chia seeds, along with the sugar and vanilla. Whisk with a hand-held electric whisk until well combined.

In a separate medium bowl, combine the chickpea (gram) flour, baking powder and salt. Add these dry ingredients to the wet ingredients and mix to combine everything using a rubber spatula. (Your cookie batter will be slightly wetter than a typical cookie batter, but don't worry.) Stir in the chocolate chips until evenly dispersed. Place the batter in the fridge to firm up for 30–60 minutes.

Preheat the oven to 180°C (350°F) Gas 4.

Scoop the chilled mixture into ping pong-sized balls, using a spoon, and space evenly apart on the prepared baking sheet. Press each cookie gently using a piece of baking parchment and your hand to flatten them slightly. Sprinkle each cookie with a small pinch of sea salt (if using).

Bake in the preheated oven for 11–12 minutes (if they look a little underdone, that's okay). Remove from the oven and leave to cool on the baking sheet for 5–10 minutes before transferring to a wire rack to cool fully. Store in an airtight container at room temperature for up to 5 days.

BAKED STRAWBERRY, BANANA AND OAT SQUARES

These fruit-filled oaty squares are delicious served warm as dessert with vegan ice cream or coconut yogurt with extra maple syrup. Leftovers served cold also make excellent on-the-go afternoon snacks.

2 tablespoons ground chia seeds

6 tablespoons water

190 g/2 cups rolled/old-fashioned oats

50 g/½ cup ground almonds

2 teaspoons ground cinnamon

1 teaspoon baking powder

¼ teaspoon salt

2 ripe bananas, roughly chopped

375 ml/1½ cups almond milk

60 ml/¼ cup pure maple syrup

3 tablespoons melted coconut oil

2 teaspoons pure vanilla extract

450 g/1 lb. strawberries, sliced

60 g/¾ cup flaked/sliced almonds

TO SERVE

coconut yogurt or vegan ice cream

pure maple syrup (optional)

20-cm/8-inch square baking pan, greased with coconut oil

SERVES 7–9

Preheat the oven to 190°C (375°F) Gas 5.

In a medium bowl, make a 'chia egg' mixture by mixing the chia seeds and water together. Let the mixture stand for 5 minutes.

In another medium bowl, combine the oats, ground almonds, cinnamon, baking powder and salt.

In the 'chia egg' bowl, mash the bananas with a fork. Add the milk, maple syrup, coconut oil and vanilla. Mix well to combine.

Add the dry ingredients to the wet ingredients and stir to combine.

Add half of the sliced strawberries and 40 g/½ cup of the flaked/sliced almonds to the mixture, and pour everything evenly into the prepared baking pan.

Top with rows of the remaining strawberry slices and sprinkle the rest of the flaked/sliced almonds over the top. Bake in the preheated oven for 35–40 minutes until set. Cut into portions.

Serve warm or at room temperature with coconut yogurt or vegan ice cream and more maple syrup, if you like it sweeter. Store in an airtight container in the fridge for up to 5 days.

CHOCOLATE BANANA BREAD

Until I met my husband, banana-flavoured anything just wasn't my thing. Somehow his love of a banana-chocolate pairing rubbed off on me, and I find myself in the mood for this banana bread all the time. I like to serve it like cake - warm and à la mode, but you can definitely eat this for breakfast too - it's free of refined sugar and high in fibre - and a little scattering of chocolate never ruined anyone's morning!

130 g/1 cup whole-wheat flour

100 g/1 cup almond flour

50 g/½ cup oat flour (or 70 g/ generous ½ cup oats, finely ground)

3 teaspoons baking powder

1 teaspoon ground cinnamon

½ teaspoon ground nutmeg

½ teaspoon salt

3 large bananas (overripe is best)

90 ml/⅓ cup melted coconut oil, plus extra for greasing

60 ml/¼ cup almond milk

1 teaspoon vanilla extract

60 ml/¼ cup pure maple syrup

80 g/½ cup dark/bittersweet vegan chocolate chips or roughly chopped chocolate

30 g/¼ cup pecans or walnuts

nut butter or vegan ice cream, to serve (optional)

12 x 23-cm/9 x 5-inch loaf pan, greased with coconut oil

MAKES 1 LOAF

Preheat the oven to 180°C (350°F) Gas 4.

Mix together the dry ingredients (flours, baking powder, spices and salt) in a medium bowl.

Mash the bananas in another bowl, then add the melted coconut oil, almond milk, vanilla and maple syrup and mix everything together using a rubber spatula.

Gradually mix the dry ingredients into the banana mixture until everything is well combined. Fold in the chocolate chips.

Pour the batter into the prepared loaf pan and sprinkle the top with the pecans or walnuts. Bake the loaf in the preheated oven for 45–50 minutes, rotating halfway through the cooking time.

Remove from the oven and leave to cool to room temperature in the pan before turning out. Serve toasted with nut butter for breakfast, or warm with vegan ice cream for dessert.

STRAWBERRY CRUMBLE CUPS

Crumbles are an easy way to cook with seasonal fruit, or to use sub-par fruit that might not quite be in season yet. The time in the oven will make it sweeter and softer and the nutty topping adds a crunchy contrast in texture. Roasted strawberries in particular, taste like straight-up candy – no extra sugar needed – making them the perfect base for a low-maintenance crumble. Serve these with a little coconut cream or vegan ice cream. I like to make a double batch of the crumble topping and store it in the freezer to top seasonal fruit with on a whim for a fast dessert fix.

200 g/2 cups strawberries, sliced into 1.5-cm/ ½-inch thick pieces

100 g/1 cup almond flour

50 g/½ cup rolled/ old-fashioned oats

½ teaspoon ground cinnamon

pinch of salt

60 ml/¼ cup gently melted coconut oil, plus extra for greasing

1 tablespoon pure maple syrup

Coconut Whipped Cream (see page 14) or vegan ice cream, to serve

4 small ramekins, greased with coconut oil

baking sheet, lined with foil or baking parchment

SERVES 4

Preheat the oven to 180°C (350°F) Gas 4.

Divide the strawberries between the ramekins, fitting them in snugly (they will reduce a little as they cook).

In a medium mixing bowl, combine the almond flour, oats, cinnamon and salt. Add the melted coconut oil and maple syrup and mix until everything is well coated. Divide the crumble mixture between the four greased ramekins, packing it tightly.

Put the ramekins on the prepared baking sheet and bake in the preheated oven for 30–35 minutes, until the strawberries are bubbling at the edges and the crumble toppings are golden and crispy.

Remove from the oven and leave to cool for 15–20 minutes before serving with coconut whipped cream or vegan ice cream.

POACHED APPLES with maple pecans

Simple juice-poached cinnamon apples make the most of natural sweetness. Serve these warm with the creamy topping of your choice and don't skip the maple pecans – they're super easy and make for good snacking if you have some leftover.

2 sweet apples (I would use Honeycrisp or Pink Lady for this)

½ teaspoon ground cinnamon

235–350 ml/1–1½ cups unfiltered apple juice

40 g/⅓ cup pecans, roughly chopped

1 teaspoon coconut oil

1 teaspoon pure maple syrup

vegan ice cream or yogurt, to serve (optional)

SERVES 4

Preheat the oven to 180°C (350°F) Gas 4.

Cut the apples in half widthways and scoop out the seeds in the centre with a spoon to create a little well. Sprinkle the white apple flesh with cinnamon.

In a small roasting pan with high sides (I use a 20 x 20-cm/8 x 8-inch one), place the apples face-down and pour in the apple juice, making sure that it covers the entire base of the roasting pan and comes a quarter to a third of the way up the apples. Bake in the preheated oven for 45–55 minutes until the apples are tender.

Meanwhile, toast the pecans in a dry frying pan/skillet over a medium-low heat for about 4–5 minutes, tossing a few times, until fragrant and beginning to turn golden.

Move the pecans to one side of the pan to clear a little space. Add the coconut oil and allow to melt. Add the maple syrup and stir into the oil using a rubber spatula (it should be bubbling a bit). Stir to combine and evenly coat the pecans. Remove from the heat and transfer the pecans onto a piece of baking parchment. Leave to cool and set fully before serving (I pop them in the fridge to speed the cooling time if the kitchen is warm).

Serve the poached apples topped with the pecans and vegan ice cream or yogurt.

SWEET POTATO CHOCOLATE MOUSSE

I was very surprised by these little cups of mousse when I first made them. They were so easy to throw together (just seven ingredients all in one bowl!) and the flavour was just what I was looking for – dark chocolatey and lightly sweetened. This mousse is more true to a dense (yet fluffy) chocolate mousse than other avocado-based versions. I love portioning them into little jars for a snack or dessert to grab throughout the week – they keep well in the fridge for 5–6 days. I like to serve them with a little sprinkle of sea salt and coconut whipped cream, if I have it.

1 large sweet potato, scrubbed clean

5 tablespoons good-quality cocoa powder

60 ml/¼ cup pure maple syrup

3 tablespoons coconut cream

1 tablespoon coconut oil

1 tablespoon ground chia seeds

sprinkle of flaky sea salt, to serve

2 small sterilized jars or glasses (optional)

SERVES 2

Preheat the oven to 200°C (400°F) Gas 6.

Poke the sweet potato with a fork a few times, place on the oven rack, and bake in the preheated oven for 45–60 minutes, or until it's soft when you squeeze it.

Remove from the oven and allow the the sweet potato to cool in the foil. Once cool, peel the skin off (it should come off easily now).

Put the sweet potato flesh into a medium-sized bowl and mash roughly with a fork to break it up.

Mix in the remaining ingredients (apart from the sea salt to serve) using a wooden spoon or a hand-held electric whisk, until smooth. For the fluffiest, best results, I use a hand-held electric whisk.

Portion into small jars or glasses and place in the fridge for at least an hour or overnight. Sprinkle the mousses with flaky sea salt when you are ready to serve.

TIRAMISU OVERNIGHT OAT PARFAIT

The killer combo of coffee and chocolate is what makes the traditional Italian dessert so craveable, but this vegan version definitely also hits the spot in a slightly more nutritious way. This recipe is equally good for dessert or breakfast as a powerful way to kick-start your day. I save the leftover coffee in my French press in a jar in the fridge to make this.

95 g/1 cup rolled/old-fashioned oats

2 tablespoons ground flax seeds/ linseeds

2 tablespoons cacao powder

pinch of sea salt

125 ml/½ cup freshly brewed coffee, cooled

125 ml/½ cup almond or coconut milk

1–2 tablespoons pure maple syrup

OPTIONAL TOPPINGS
Coconut Whipped Cream (page 14) or plain soy yogurt

grated dark/bittersweet vegan chocolate, or cacao powder

SERVES 2

Combine the oats, flax seeds/linseeds, cacao powder and sea salt in a jar with a lid and mix to combine. Add the coffee, milk of choice and maple syrup, and stir well. Pop the lid on and place in the refrigerator overnight.

When you are ready to serve, top the parfait with coconut cream or soy yogurt and grated chocolate or cacao powder.

CHOCOLATE PEANUT BUTTER CHIA POTS

Cacao is great for natural energy, high in antioxidants and unequivocally a health food. Here I combine it with chia and peanut butter for a protein- and omega-3-packed breakfast-meets-pudding situation.

500 ml/2 cups coconut milk (see Note)

4 tablespoons cacao powder

3 tablespoons pure maple syrup (or more to taste)

3 tablespoons peanut butter, plus extra to serve

¼ teaspoon sea salt

80 g/½ cup chia seeds

OPTIONAL SUPERFOOD AND SUPERSPICE ADD-INS
1 teaspoon maca powder

½ teaspoon ashwagandha

1 teaspoon ground cinnamon

OPTIONAL TOPPINGS
fresh raspberries or strawberries

cacao nibs or vegan dark/ bittersweet chocolate chunks

SERVES 4–6

Mix the coconut milk, cacao powder, maple syrup, peanut butter and salt (if you're using any superfoods or spices, add them now) together in a large bowl and blend with a whisk or a stick blender until you have a chocolate-y, peanut butter-y milk.

In a large jar with a lid, combine the chia seeds with the chocolate peanut butter smoothie, stir to combine, then cover and refrigerate overnight.

In the morning (or within a few hours), you'll have a thick, chocolate mousse-like mixture. Spoon into bowls or glasses to serve. Top with berries, a drizzle of peanut butter and some cacao nibs (or chocolate chunks!) to serve.

Note: Look for cans of organic, guar gum-free full-fat coconut milk (ideally, the only ingredients should be coconut and water). The texture can be thick, so I combine a 400-g/14-oz. can with 250 ml/1 cup of filtered water and keep it in a jar in my refrigerator to use throughout the week, or in a recipe such as this one.

AQUAFABA PAVLOVA with fresh fruit

Aquafaba is the water that chickpeas are cooked in. This ingredient amazingly acts like egg whites in many dishes, making it a great plant-based substitution in a pavlova. This recipe can be a bit of a diva – whipping times can vary and the aquafaba has to be properly chilled. However, the prep is pretty easy if you have all your ducks in a row. Your end result should have a crispy outer shell with a slightly hollow, soft, almost marshmallowy inside. Don't worry if your pavlova deflates a little after cooking, you're going to top it with cream and fresh fruit anyway.

150 g/¾ cup caster/superfine sugar

2 tablespoons arrowroot powder or cornflour/ cornstarch

pinch of salt

liquid from 1 x 400-g/14-oz. can of no-added salt (low sodium) organic chickpeas, chilled in the fridge overnight

1 teaspoon apple cider vinegar

1 teaspoon vanilla extract

TO SERVE

Coconut Whipped Cream (see page 14)

220 g/1½ cups fresh fruit (I like berries, sliced peaches or mangoes)

icing/confectioners' sugar for dusting (optional)

large baking sheet, lined with baking parchment

SERVES 6–8

Preheat the oven to 150°C (300°F) Gas 2.

Place a large mixing bowl in the freezer for a few minutes to make it extra cold. In another bowl, combine the sugar, arrowroot (or cornflour/cornstarch) and salt.

In the large chilled bowl, put the chilled aquafaba liquid (straight out of the fridge) and vinegar and beat with a hand-held electric whisk or in a stand mixer at a medium speed for about 2–4 minutes, until soft peaks begin to form, scraping down the sides of the bowl once or twice.

While still mixing, start adding the sugar mixture, one spoonful at a time. When all the sugar has been added, beat for about 3–6 minutes until stiff, glossy peaks form. You should be able to turn the bowl upside down without the mixture moving at the end of whipping. Add the vanilla and beat for another 10 seconds.

Tip the mixture onto the prepared baking sheet and form into a 20-cm/8-inch wide circle using a rubber spatula. Leave space around the edges, as it will spread a bit.

Put in the oven and immediately lower the heat to 120°C (250°F) Gas ½. Bake for 1½–2 hours until the outer shell is hardened when you tap it. Turn off the heat and allow the pavlova to cool completely inside the closed oven – sometimes I'll make it at night and leave it there until the morning. When ready, top with whipped coconut cream, fruit and icing/confectioners' sugar and serve immediately.

INDEX

PICTURE CREDITS

All photography by Clare Winfield apart from:

Peter Cassidy
page 74

Tara Fisher
page 56

Mowie Kay
page 122

Steve Painter
page 74

William Reavell
pages 9, 10, 94

Matt Russell
Endpapers